Life After Losing A Child ...

A Mother's Grief and Spiritual Journey

By Glenda Beebout Pyzer

Life After Losing a Child

© 2015, 2016 by Glenda Beebout Pyzer

Edited by Susan Stout

Dedication

I dedicate this book to my son, Ryan.

You have shown me, in so many ways, that you have been holding onto me in this storm. Although your presence is in a different form now, you are most definitely still here. My deep and pure love for you led me on a journey, and in that journey, you repeatedly showed me that love knows no boundaries. Love, the greatest gift we are given, has the power to bridge Heaven and Earth. I thank you for giving me courage to search, nurturing my faith each step of the way, and for leading me through a spiritual door that has changed my life forever. It is because of you and your unconditional love for me that I write this book now. May my story, and the love which inspired me to share it, help others on their journeys.

Acknowledgements

*I thank my husband, Russ, for standing by my side through the pain, my spiritual awakening, writing my blog and the endless support in writing this book. His belief in me when spiritual doors opened freed me to keep searching for more understanding. His love, support and encouragement through this journey has been a sacred gift to me.

*I thank all of my kids. Their love for their brother has been a blessing to witness. They have grieved deeply, received signs from Ryan of his presence and have shared in my spiritual journey with an unwavering faith. I know Ryan is grateful and so very proud of them.

*I thank my mom for being right there for me when I lost Ryan, putting her own health issues on hold. She always seemed to know what to do along the way to ease my heart. She created a memorial fund for Ryan, for which I will forever be grateful. She also shared in my spiritual journey with acceptance, faith and encouragement. I also thank my dad for coming to me in a dream two nights before Ryan died. He let me know he would be there for Ryan, which helped ease my heart from questioning myself about the things "I should have done or known" by showing me it was Ryan's time before it happened. I miss them both.

*I thank my sister and brothers. They all came immediately when they found out Ryan died, and they continue to be at my side. They speak of Ryan with love, and without hesitation, which is exactly what I continue to need. They have been a loving support and comfort for me and for my family. They continue to show me what family is all about.

*I thank my brother Stephen for seeing the gifts I was given long before I even recognized them. He has been a great champion of my gifts and has encouraged their development from the beginning. When spiritual things began to happen to me, he was my safe haven and "go to guy." He never doubted, but rather cheered me on to develop them further. He also has never missed the opportunity to say, "I told you so!"

*I thank my dear friend, Becky. Through sharing her own pain and journey, she opened spiritual doors for me that I one day would walk through. Her belief in me, as spiritual gifts opened, has been steadfast and she has been a great supporter of my writing. She has encouraged me to be honest, no matter what people may think. Her belief in me has helped me to believe in

4

myself. She has a magical way of calming my soul. Because of our shared experiences, we have a very special friendship, and I am so very grateful for her powerful presence in my life.

*I thank sweet Lance. In the gifts he has given to his mom, he has given hope and faith to me. He has gently touched my soul and that imprint will be with me always. I also thank him for being such a good and loving friend to Ryan.

*I thank my friends Kathy, Nancy, Lori and Sandi for supporting me in my spiritual journey. They all have a different, yet very special, place in my heart. They have all shared in my spiritual experiences, supporting and encouraging this path I am on since it first began. They have all enthusiastically encouraged my writing — Kathy and Lori since we were in college! They have helped lift me when I didn't know if I had the strength to stand alone. I will never forget that.

*I thank my friend Dr. Winston Vaughan. He started out as my doctor and quickly became my friend. Since Ryan's death, he has supported me, encouraged me, and my writing, and continually insisted my path was to help other parents. I didn't know what that meant for me, but I knew his words were true. I now understand part of that path is this book. I hope he understands how important his friendship has been to me in this journey I am on, and how grateful I am to have him in my life.

*I thank the other close friends in my life (they know who they are) for being there to support me when Ryan died, and continuing to support me in that loss. I thank them for always believing in me and the power of my words, and encouraging me to help other parents through my blog, and now this book.

Prelude

On September 22, 2010, I lost my 16-year-old son, Ryan. He died in his sleep. We found out through an autopsy that the cause was acute hemorrhagic pancreatitis. After more physical examination, they found no physical cause for the fatal attack. The coroner determined it must have been a bacteria or virus that caused the inflammation. We were all in shock. A healthy, athletic boy was gone. Why?

The loss of Ryan shook me to my very core. I have endured many losses in my life, but how was I supposed to survive the loss of my own child? The day it happened, I was instantly changed. I didn't know what that meant, I just knew I was not the same person I was the day before, and would never be that person again. That left me feeling very unsure, afraid and alone.

Within a month of Ryan's death, I decided I needed to write. I wanted to release and process the pain, as well as document the journey I was taking. I wasn't sure why, but I knew I needed to do it. I decided to start a blog: http://glendapyzer.blogspot.com I had never composed a blog before, although I did have a passion for writing. I am also a very private person, especially with my own heartaches, so this was totally out of character for me. Writing to release my feelings is very normal for me, but to put it on a public forum was completely foreign to me. I felt compelled to put it all down in a blog rather than a journal. I knew the reason must be bigger than me, bigger than my sadness. So I listened to that calling, which I felt was coming from God, knowing if I somehow helped others, I would come to understand.

I immediately got feedback from friends, who gave me the courage to keep writing. Each time I wrote, my heart felt relief. Within a very short period of time, I started receiving emails from other parents all over the United States and Canada who had experienced the loss of a child. They told me my blog was helping them, that my words were what their hearts felt. I have become friends with some of these people and I am so grateful for that. I now understand why I was led to create and write my blog.

During the time I was blogging, many spiritual things began to happen. I did not bring them to the blog, out of fear of what people would think. I was doing a lot of reading and personal searching. I have always had a strong faith in God and life after death; but when you lose a child, knowing he is in heaven is not good enough. You want and need to understand what that looks like, what it all means. I read books written by people who lost their children. I also read books and articles by people who have had near-death experiences, and I read books by mediums.

Although I believed life went on after our time here on Earth, and the people we loved would watch over us, I never thought about what that must be like or whether we could communicate with them. I felt we could be given signs, and I'm sure many people have experienced that. Growing up and going to church, no one talked about communication with people who have died, with spirits. I wasn't told they could communicate with us; however, I wasn't told they couldn't. I never judged those who believed we could communicate, and I never judged those who felt we couldn't. I simply didn't give it much thought. That all changed when I lost Ryan.

During my journey of searching, I began simple meditations. My son was gone; I saw the signs being sent, but I needed to find him. I'm his mom. Those simple meditations opened doors I couldn't believe. I was amazed at what I was seeing, feeling and hearing. I found Ryan, and I found so much more. My faith is stronger than ever before. God's Grace has poured over me and the gifts from that have been so healing.

This book is about my grief as a mother and my journey through the pain. I have included many blog entries as they were so important in my voyage, giving me a way to express my vulnerable, grieving heart. At times I will go into more detail with the entries; at times the blog entry will say it all. Even though I know life goes on, I am still human. My heart still aches for my son. I have had to find ways to learn to live with the loss and survive particularly hard times like birthdays and holidays. No matter what I believe, this pain is something I am destined to carry forever.

This book is also about my spiritual journey. I am not afraid of what people think anymore. I know what is real, and it's time to share that with other parents who are broken. I have been blessed with gifts, witnessed communications and experienced amazing things. If my blog helped other parents, I can only believe this book will do the same. It is not only about the grief and living with the loss; it's about the fact that we don't die. Our children and loved ones are still with us, are communicating with us, and we will see them again. In that reality I have found healing, hope, faith and promise. It is my sincere hope, that in sharing my story, you will find the same.

Chapter 1

Tragedy Strikes

Blog Entry:

Sunday, October 24, 2010

The Day My Life Changed Forever

It was September 22, 2010. The day started like any other, but events would unfold which would forever change the woman I am. At 9:35 a.m. I received a phone call that literally took my breath away. My husband was on the phone, sobbing, telling me that my son Ryan was not breathing. The first thing I asked him was if Ryan felt cold ... the answer shook my soul. I remember bending over in anguish, saying, "I can't do this" as my friend stood by to be sure I could. We immediately left the classroom and my friend drove me toward home, not knowing where they would take Ryan. On that drive, the longest drive of my life, I talked to my husband numerous times. Each time he informed me they were still working on Ryan and finally told me where they would be taking him. I then called Ryan's dad and brother, who immediately were on their way. We arrived at the hospital before Ryan, so I waited for the ambulance. I will never forget the sound of the distant sirens, knowing they were sounding so they could bring me my son. As I watched the ambulance pull in, I walked to the doors so I could see my baby. They pulled him out, while I watched them continue to push his chest and pump breaths into his lifeless body. I will never forget that image. Within 10 minutes, a doctor came out in tears, and told me they couldn't save him. I knew in my heart he had died prior to arriving, so this news confirmed my instincts. I immediately went in to see him. A breathing tube still inserted, he lay there, motionless. I could not believe this was happening. Not My Ryan ...

I remembered a dream I had two nights before and knew the answer to my question was right in front of me. I had a dream with my dad, who had died almost 12 years prior. I have often asked to dream of him, as I wanted so badly to see him again. But in all these years, not one dream blessed my sleep. On September 19, my dad came to me. There was a white door in front of me. I opened the door, and there stood my dad. In my dream I did not know he was dead, but I did have incredible feelings of joy when I saw him. He stood smiling at me, in his usual attire, hair combed nicely, as if he were going to church. I remember looking at him and thinking how wonderful he looked. He had never looked better and, in my eyes, was actually radiating beauty. It was amazing. I invited him in to "meet our newest one" and picked a baby off a bed. I laid the baby in his arms. He smiled, and I woke up. For the next two days I tried to figure out who I was handing to my dad, as I knew the dream meant something. As I stood and looked at my Ryan in the hospital, I realized instantly I had placed my baby, Ryan, into my dad's arms.

I went outside, and again, I phoned his dad in route. I will never forget the painful cries I heard over the phone as I shared what had happened. I called my mom, who immediately went to my house to take care of the younger kids. I waited outside, as my husband was bringing my daughter Kaitie, and I needed to tell her what happened. When they pulled in, she walked toward me in fear, and I told her. She began crying and I held her in her pain, trying so hard not to show my own. My friend took my girls home, and I went back in to be with Ryan. I cried, I touched his soft face, rubbed his thick hair I loved so much, lifted his eyelids so I could look into his eyes one last time, and held his hand. Tears streamed down my face as I sat there in total disbelief. Shortly after, Ryan's dad and his girlfriend, and my 20-year-old son arrived. My son was so angry, yelling at the nurses for not doing their job. His pain, as he looked at his brother lying there, was piercing to my heart. He went outside, and my husband followed him.

We took care of "the business" that needed to be taken care of, and we went home — home to a house full of family, friends, love and support. Some of his friends, in painful tears, stopped by. I held them all, somehow finding strength within so I could comfort them. They were so loving, so hurt, so young. When they left, I went into my house so full of people, yet it felt so empty. I was forever a changed woman.

13

I was in complete shock that day. I felt stunned, yet surprisingly attentive, to the things that had to be done before I could go home, the home where Ryan took his last breath. I didn't know if I even wanted to be there. Ryan's dad and I went to the mortuary and made all of the initial arrangements. We did what had to be done. I suppose that is all either of us was capable of doing. As I drove home alone in my car, I cried and kept wondering in my mind if it was really happening. *How could this be? How do I go home? How could a home without Ryan ever be a home again?* I was completely lost, with no sense of belonging anywhere. When I finally pulled into my driveway, my front yard was full of people. I'm not sure who all was there. I initially saw my mom, who I called from the hospital. I knew she would help hold my life together if I couldn't. My brothers and sister were all there. They drove over an hour each to be there and I will never forget that. For weeks, my mom came over daily; my brothers for days, and my sister stayed at the house for a few days. These people would prove to be my greatest supporters as time went on.

Blog Entry:

Sunday, October 24, 2010

Candlelight Vigils

The day Ryan died, Piner High School in Santa Rosa held a candlelight vigil in the parking lot. There must have been 200 kids there with candles. They shared stories, memories, nicknames given to them by Ryan, and above all, they shared about Ryan's heart. I heard stories of Ryan reaching out to kids

14

hurting, kids who were new to the school and kids he had never met before. These kids talked about my boy for 90 minutes! In the crowd were people from all walks of life. Ryan did not care about grades, the crowd someone hung out in, race, or gender. He saw into each person's heart and was a friend with everyone. All you had to do was look into the crowd of people and you instantly knew what kind of heart Ryan had. The same thing held true Friday night following his passing, when they had a candlelight vigil for Ryan at Middletown High School. About 100 kids, again very diverse in population. He loved WITHOUT passing judgment on others — I know so many adults who could learn an important lesson from Ryan! Ryan loved others the way we are told to love, the way we are called to love. He was a 16-year-old who walked around telling everyone, "One Love." He believed in God, in peace, in brotherhood, in union, in love, and in each person's heart. I knew my baby had a good and loving heart; I just didn't know he was touching so many with his love.

The vigils were so touching, painful and uplifting. Ryan was so loved, and he gave love so freely to others. Hearing stories of what he had done for others, things I had no idea about, somehow brought great peace to my heart. As we drove home, I kept wondering if all of it was really happening. *How could this be?* I slept in his bed that night, and for many nights to follow. I needed to be in the place he was before he died, the place where he took his last breath.

As I lay in his bed, I kept replaying the day. Every detail ran through my mind relentlessly. I felt so alone, so afraid and so unsure of how I would ever survive this. *What just happened? How could my Ryan be gone? How was I supposed to continue on, living without him? Who am I now?* I know I'm not the same person I was yesterday. *How will my children get through this? How will I be able to help them? How did he die? Why did he die? Is this really happening?*

Blog Entry:

Sunday, October 24, 2010

The Physical Goodbyes

September 24, 2010, was the day that my family saw Ryan for the last time here on Earth. I went early so I could dress him. I was the first person in his life to dress him and felt a very strong need to be the last. Seeing the scars from the autopsy was not easy, but I was taking care of my little boy, so I endured. It was very important for me that his brothers and sisters not see the scars but see the brother they love, so I dressed him in a black T-shirt and a pair of jean shorts. He looked just like my Ryan always looked, in a sad sort of way. Before everyone got there I had Father Ryan, an old family friend, come and bless my baby. He prayed over him, blessed him, and we prayed together. Ryan would have liked that. When the family came in, there were tears, anguish, hugs, despair ... a pain I could not take away or make better. We all were carrying it, in our own ways. Each person took their turn and went up to be with Ryan and say whatever his or her heart needed to say — very tender moments for each person, very painful and very private. I went up when everyone left and spent time with my baby. How was a mother supposed to walk away and leave her child with strangers? How was I supposed to go home, knowing he would not be there? How was I to leave him, knowing I would never hold him again or hear his sweet voice? How is a mother supposed to do this?

Sunday, October 24, 2010

I NEEDED to see Him One Last Time

When your baby dies, nothing is right. So many decisions to make, so quickly they need to be made. Planning for your child in death is something you never think about, nor should you have to.

We decided to cremate Ryan, which was a choice I knew was right. Just before Mother's Day, we lost our dog, Ryan's dog, Lucky. I was going to bury him in our backyard but Ryan had a violent reaction to the idea. He thought it was depressing to bury him in the ground and asked if we could cremate him and bring the ashes home. To him this was the right way to handle things. I honored his wishes, but in retrospect, I somehow feel he was laying out his own wishes for the future. I honored his wishes again.

I had the urgency to see my little boy one last time. I needed to see him in the last spot his body would be upon this Earth. This happened to be at the foot of the crematory, but it didn't matter; I needed to see him one last time.

My mom went with me. It was not easy, by any means. Laying on him were the two roses my sister had bought for the two of us to give him. In his pocket, a note from his brother. I put his report card in his pocket ... a 3.5 GPA which would have gotten him his driver's license. I was so proud, so I wrote a note on it for him. I was also so sad as he didn't get to celebrate what he told me he was going to do ... get his license. I also put a copy of the poem I had written to him in his pocket.

As I stood there, tears just streamed down my face. I held his hand, ran my hands through his gorgeous hair, rubbed his thick eyebrows, and held his beautiful face in my hands for the last time. My little boy was gone, and I could not wrap my head around

17

it. The pain was all-consuming. I turned to walk out, and as I did, I heard the squeak of the door opening ... the door which led to my little boy's cremation. My heart dropped. I will never forget that sound; but more so, I will never forget my little boy lying there, lifeless, as I held his face in my hands. Again I wondered ... how is a mother supposed to do this?

I will never forget that day, the day tragedy struck. In my lifetime, I never imagined I would ever lose a child. Who does? That's not the way it's supposed to be. A parent should never bury his or her child. But sadly, we do. The pain of that kind of loss is so piercing there are no words to describe it. It just is. It leaves you feeling so alone, unsure and isolated. You watch the people around you who are also hurting, but you realize they cannot begin to understand the pain you are feeling. No one, except another parent who has lost a child, can really understand.

That night, and many nights to follow, I slept in Ryan's bed, the place he took his last breath. I needed to be close to him, and somehow this brought him closer. I looked around his room, taking note of every detail, knowing each item was in the place that he last put it. As I lay there, I wondered what he was experiencing as he died. *Was he in pain?* That thought almost pushed me over the edge because, as his mother, I needed to protect him. *Was there something I could have done? How did I not see this coming?* And always the same questions: *is this really happening and how am I supposed to live life without Ryan here?*

18

Thursday, October 26, 2010

Relentless Questioning

When you lose someone, anyone, you are often left with questions of how you could have changed things, prevented things, or done things differently. When you lose a child, the questions are relentless, cutting so sharply into your heart. Whether it's an accident, a suicide or natural causes, as a mother you are flooded with questions. As a mother your job is to love, nurture and protect your children from harm. When one dies, somehow you have failed him. Ryan died of acute hemorrhagic pancreatitis. The medical examiner told me he could not have eaten dinner if this had started before bed. In his opinion, Ryan had a perfectly healthy pancreas, and in a matter of several hours, it had failed him. He assured me there was nothing I could have done and no way to know. My first question to the doctor, as I cried in fear: was he hurting? As his mom, I couldn't handle the idea that my little boy was hurting and I was not there to help him. To hold him. No one can say for sure, but it is assumed because his pancreas was failing, his sugar levels went so high he probably went into a coma and didn't know what was happening. As much as my head tells me this is probably true, my heart still questions. Was there something I could have done? Did he know what was happening? Was he scared? Why didn't my motherly instincts tell me something was wrong? Why didn't they tell me my baby had died? My son died alone, in his bed, and I find that very hard. In my head I know he wouldn't have chosen a different place. He loved his room, his bed, and living with me. He told me this many times. I just need my heart to embrace what my head knows already, but for whatever reason, this is not easy to do. The questions run relentlessly through my heart. I know we all wish we could have a peaceful death ... to die in our sleep sounds like a gift. But in my heart, a mother's heart, I knew my baby was alone and I wish I could have been holding him as he went from my arms into my dad's. Hold him in My Love, as God took him into His.

When someone dies we often beat ourselves up with wondering what we could have done differently or with regrets of how we treated that person. I was very grateful that the latter was not in my mind at all. I had a great relationship with my son. He knew how much I loved him and we would talk about relationships, struggles and anything else our hearts wanted to share with each other. I had no regrets, just memories filled with love. However, as his mother, I began to question his health. I tried to recall every time he said his stomach hurt. It wasn't often, but when you are faced with this, every moment in time is analyzed. *Why didn't I take him to the doctor? Was this a condition he had and I didn't recognize it?* As I would start to spiral into the realms of failing my son, I was reminded of the dream I mentioned in my first blog, the dream in which I handed my baby to my dad. I would remind myself that this dream happened before Ryan's death. Therefore, what happened to Ryan was going to happen. It was his time. There was nothing anyone could do to change that. I felt very grateful to my dad for coming to me in that dream. I am convinced my dad was doing that for two reasons: One, to let me know he would be there to meet my baby; Two, so I wouldn't relentlessly beat myself up with questions of how I could have changed things to save Ryan from his death; it was his time to go, and we don't have the power to change the plan. This is a natural road for a parent to go down. I feel so grateful that my dad

20

stepped in to try and ease some of my heartache and keep me from going down the path of self-destruction. This was the beginning of a spiritual road I would soon embark upon, a spiritual road I will share later in this book.

Blog Entry:

Sunday, October 24, 2010

Working on the Memorial Kept Me Breathing

On September 25, 2010, I was already working on plans for the Memorial. I needed a reason to breathe, and honoring my little boy in the way I felt he deserved to be honored kept me breathing for the next 3 weeks. The first thing I did was write a poem for his Memorial Card. It poured out of my heart in the late hours of the night, so I typed it up and checked one job off the list. Next was finding a place to hold the Memorial, which ended up being at the church I took Ryan to when we lived in Santa Rosa. He loved that church. It was very alive and nurturing. That job was done.

Now for the date ... after many calls to and from the church, the date which we came up with was October 15, the anniversary of the death of my grandmother (my dad's mom). My dad completely loved his mother, and she loved him. I think they shared the kind of love Ryan and I shared. Since my dad came to get Ryan in my dream, I knew this date was somehow part of the plan. I'm not sure what it all means, or the reasons God has, but I know this date was part of the plan He already had laid out.

Back to work ... Ryan's dad agreed to take care of the food, working with the church, so that was something I didn't have to worry about. I just told him I wanted LOTS of food as Ryan would love that; my boy LOVED eating! I started collecting pictures from a photo album I had made for Ryan. I had

21

started one for each of my kids when they were born, so that when they were adults, I could give them an album or two of themselves during their early years. My daughter Shawndre' came over one night and together we picked pictures from these albums. I then moved to all the pictures I had on the computer, as well as going through photos that his dad's girlfriend had given me. I literally spent hours choosing photos, arranging them, and picking the perfect songs for sending my little boy off — Love songs from me to him, yet songs that would hold meaning to all who cared to listen. Most important, I knew Ryan would be listening and he would know why each song was chosen and why pictures played as they did. Honoring Ryan was all I cared about during those 3 weeks. Since meaningful music was carrying my heavy heart, I decided to make a CD to play prior to the service and at the reception. I took songs from everywhere, and everyone, once again choosing songs that spoke from my heart. The last thing to do was write my eulogy. This was the hardest thing I have ever written. What do I say? Will I be able to even speak? All I knew was I had to do this. I had to do it for Ryan, and from that powerful love is where my strength came. The memorial was beautiful. There were about 500 people there, once again from all walks of life. The tributes to Ryan were all beautiful and heartfelt. Tears were shed, hearts ached. The slideshow came off beautifully. There was an abundance of food for everyone, which is how Ryan would have wanted it. We honored Ryan just as I wanted it to be. I couldn't have sent him off with any more love or respect. I was grateful to all who came, to all who helped, to God for guiding me through the previous 3 weeks, and to Ryan, for standing beside me as I spoke of him. I asked him to help me get through it, and he did. My baby was there for me.

The next day when I awoke I was filled with emptiness and sadness. I gave my baby everything I had; now I was left with the reality that he was gone. I was broken. I am broken.

Blog Entry:

Sunday, November 7, 2010

A Mother's Eulogy

As I write this, a public goodbye and respect to my Ryan, I wonder what a mother is supposed to say when she has lost her child. What is too much? What is not enough? But even more than this, I wonder why any mother should have to lose her child.

Ryan was so much ... to so many. He was a son, a brother, a grandson, a nephew, a cousin, a godson, and a friend. But for me, Ryan was my baby. He was my infant, my toddler, my little boy, my teenager. He was my Ryan.

I can still remember the joy and completeness I felt each time he moved inside of me. I remember every detail of his birth like it was yesterday: my St. Patrick's Day baby with bright, red hair and big blue eyes. I remember his quiet nature as an infant, never crying or fussing. He was so quiet that I often called the pediatrician as I thought something must be wrong with him. They would always assure me he was perfectly fine, just a content and happy baby. I remember his quiet nature as a toddler and little boy, his extreme shyness at large gatherings of people, his ability to amuse himself, and the comfort he always seemed to have with being by himself. I remember the way he would fight a smile; and if one started to show, he would try to cover his mouth with his hand so no one would see. I told Ryan many times it was OK to smile, that people loved to see him smile. And when he did let you see, or he just couldn't hide the joy in his face any longer, the room simply exploded in the happiness his smile would penetrate. His smile was magical. It was a gift to me every time I saw it. From a baby to 16 years old, Ryan had a smile that brought complete joy to my heart.

23

As Ryan got older, he loved adventures and seeing new places. He loved vacations and went on many of them with his dad and me throughout the years. When on vacation with me, we would often fly. We went to the East Coast, to Disneyland many times, and to Hawaii. Every time we got to the airport Ryan would explode with excitement, which I loved to see. When we got on the plane, he would always pull out the Bible he was given my his Aunt Leslie at his baptism. The first time he did this, I asked him why he packed his Bible. His answer was simply, "I know nothing will happen to this plane if I have my Bible." He believed in God and really felt carrying the Bible would keep him safe. There was such a pure sweetness in him. We went to Disneyland last year, his Bible again in hand.

Mothers always see the good in their children. No matter what was happening with Ryan, I always saw his heart. His heart was pure. It was loving. It was giving. It was tender. It was vulnerable. Because of these qualities, I have always felt very protective of Ryan. Hearts this loving can so easily be hurt, and the last thing a mother wants is to see her child hurt. I often prayed for him at night, asking God to protect him, fill him, and guide him always. Because of his heart, it was easy to trust him, as I always felt his heart would lead the way. I would often tell him to listen to his heart and follow where it led. Little did I know the kind of love he was spreading to all he met.

His friends were from all walks of life. Ryan didn't care if someone was an A student or if they were in trouble with the law. He didn't care about color, race, gender, or the circle of friends someone had. He saw people's hearts and loved them for that, and that alone. He didn't care what people thought of him; he was secure in himself. He told me once, "If someone judges me wrong because of someone I am friends with, that is their problem, not mine. I know my heart; I know my friend's hearts, and that's all that matters." I had great respect for his beliefs and *opinions, and because of that, I had a deep trust in him.*

Our relationship was sacred to me. We were open and honest with each other. We shared personal experiences and feelings, never judging the other. If he needed anything, he knew I was there for him. We had a pure and complete love for each other, and I will forever be grateful for that. He was literally a part of me physiually, spiritually and emotionally.

I am not the same woman I was on September 21st when I said goodnight to Ryan and told him I loved him for the last time. I know I will never be the same woman again. I don't think you can lose a child and ever go back to the way you were. It is too life-altering. I only pray that somehow I will endure this unbearable pain and emptiness, and rise again, becoming an even better person than I was before I lost him. This would be the greatest honor I could ever give my Ryan. I always gave him everything I had, and he knew it, so I wouldn't dream of stopping now.

I wrote this eulogy for Ryan on my 50th birthday. When you lose a child, you are left so helpless. Not knowing which direction to move, or if you can even move at all, you manage to face each day. I needed something very meaningful to do and it had to be about Ryan. People may think that arranging the services for your child is unbearable. In fact, it is almost a relief as it distracts you from the reality and emptiness of not having him there. As I made arrangements for Ryan's memorial, I felt his presence so strongly. I was doing everything I could to honor my son one last time, and this brought comfort to me.

I wanted to make a DVD slide show of his short life to play at the memorial. I felt it would honor his life and knew how important that was for us all. Endless hours were spent going through pictures and scanning them onto a computer. I smiled, I cried and I kept on it because it had to be perfect for Ryan. I found the right songs to capture my heart and recorded them on the computer. I literally spent hours and hours preparing for his memorial service. The last thing I did was write the eulogy I would give at his service. I had no interest in my birthday, so I spent it focusing on my Ryan. The day had to be perfect. It would be the last time we honored him and the last time I spoke to and about his importance in my life — at least that is what I thought at the time.

The memorial was perfect. We honored Ryan exactly the way I wanted it to be, the way he would have loved it to be. It was all about him and the beauty he created everywhere he went and with everyone he touched. I had spent the previous 3 weeks preparing for the day and could not have been happier with the way it turned out. The music was perfect, fitting each picture that was displayed. The eulogies given were perfect, reflecting each person's relationship with Ryan. Even though I almost fell apart a couple of times, I was able to speak at my son's memorial and honored him with my words and heart.

Since the day Ryan died, I had been going full speed to make sure the memorial was everything he deserved. Now I stood in the silence of darkness. My son was gone, the services were over, and somehow I had to figure out how to move on. I had no purpose, or so it seemed. All I had was the reality of what had just happened. For weeks I had felt close to him as I put his memorial together. Now it was over, and my heart was completely laden with pain, emptiness and sorrow.

Where do I go from here? How do I move forward? Why should I move forward? Who am I? How do I do this? Do I even want to? Again, is this really happening?

Chapter 2

Trying to Understand

Blog Entry:

Monday, October 25, 2010

Whispers from God

During the past month, God has whispered to me many times. I have always been one to have dreams, to see things, to hear the message I felt was being sent. I have felt God talk to me through other people, through music, through written words, through nature, through rainbows, through dreams. I have had some powerful dreams! My relationship with God has been alive, distant, gentle, turbulent, but always there. No matter how deep the hurt, I always believed. No matter how far away I pushed Him, I knew He was there waiting.

I have never been good at asking for help, no matter what the circumstances. But this time, I have been broken to a place where I am more than willing to accept help. I have been broken to a place where I feel helpless. People are reaching out and giving so freely and selflessly, which is amazing to me. What amazes me more is my ability to accept it. For the first time in my life, I am accepting from others without question, simply gratitude. If you know me, you know this is not typical for me. It's easy to give, hard to receive. I am also taking things very slowly as I know one step at a time is all I can handle. I have never been one to look after myself the way I should, but I find myself doing that very thing I never knew how to do. God has taken me down to my knees with pain, and down here is where I have learned to care for myself and accept from others.

During the past month, the longest month of my life, I have had whispers from God, whispers from Ryan, whispers from my dad. Just enough whispers to give me hope, to keep my faith alive, and to help me get out of bed each day. The first whisper was the dream I had about my dad before Ryan died. I think of that dream often; it helps me understand that there was a plan, even if I can't accept or understand it. It simply reminds me that my little boy is in heaven with Dad now, even though I wish he was here. I turn to the dream often just for comfort.

On the Friday when my family saw Ryan that last time (and I thought my last time), I had pleaded with Ryan to let me know he was happy and OK. That night I went to the Middletown High School vigil for Ryan. The students gave me a candle, with a card attached to the candle, which basically said, "Perhaps the stars are openings in the sky for our loved ones to shine down and let us know they are HAPPY." To top it off, at the end of the vigil, they ended by playing "Amazing Grace," which was one of my dad's favorite songs. I knew again my dad was with him, and he was letting me know it loud and clear.

I have also seen numerous heart shapes in the clouds and sky. Not a shape I have ever seen in the sky before, but I see it often now. Ryan use to say, "One Love, One Heart," so I know the hearts are Ryan letting me know he is happy and watching over us. He knows One Love now.

Rainbows, always signs for me, have been sent in my most painful moments, filling me with hope. This has happened for years. One evening a couple of weeks ago I received a text, and at the time didn't know who it was from. It had a picture of Jesus, and then a song started playing....."If I die young, bury me in satin. Lay me down on a bed of roses. Sink me in a river, at dawn, send me away with the words of a love song. Lord make me a rainbow, I'll shine down on my mother. She'll know I'm safe with you when she stands under my colors..." The song cut off right there. I knew it was another whisper — well, actually, it was more like someone yelling! I tracked down that song and put it on the CD for the memorial.

When I was working on the slideshow I had a lot of anxiety about it coming together perfectly, hoping Ryan would like it. One night I had a dream. In front of me was the computer with the slide show, the projector, and off in the distance was Ryan dancing, looking at me, and singing, "that's for me." I woke up immediately after he sang that. I knew he was letting me know he was watching and he approved!

Then, the night before the one month anniversary of Ryan's death, I pleaded with God to let me know what time Ryan died. As a mother, I needed to know. I know it was sometime before Russ found him, and I just needed that answer. That night I had a dream. I was walking along a road with tons of mailboxes. On each box were the numbers for the house I suppose. As I walked and looked at all the numbers I was passing, all of a sudden everything started to get dark, and a light shone down from the sky, lighting up 3 numbers. I knew instantly this was the time Ryan had died.

30

I woke up the next morning, the anniversary of his death, 1 minute before he had died.

These are the whispers I speak of, the shimmers of light which let me know that God knows I am hurting and He hears me. The promise He will carry me through this. The shimmers of light which let me know Ryan is watching and pouring his love over me. The shimmers of light which tell me my dad is with my baby now. Although I am so grateful for each whisper heard, and know I will plead for more, there is still nothing I want more than to have my Ryan back home with me.

The whispers from God, as powerful and beautiful as they are, do not take away the pain of a mother who has lost her child. Perhaps this is a pain which will never go away, a loss I will never get over but perhaps learn to get through.

These whispers were lifesaving during that first month. I was in such despair. It was so dark at times that I was horrified of even thinking about Ryan and living life without him here. God, Ryan, my dad and everyone else in heaven who loves me were all sending whispers to keep me moving, even if it was only one small step at a time. I grabbed onto each and every glimmer of light, knowing it was the lifeline that would save me. I had other children and a husband to help; I couldn't let myself sink into the hole I felt I was being pulled into. Although, in all honesty, sometimes I just wanted to sink into that hole and die, a truth I couldn't admit to anyone. I needed to keep moving forward. Without these whispers of hope, faith and reassurance, I know I wouldn't have made it to where I am now. They were also the whispers that helped open so many spiritual doors. Again, I will talk about that later.

Wednesday, October 27, 2010

God's Will Versus My Own

My entire life I have questioned God's will for me, for my family, and for my life. There have been so many times I had a plan, the way I felt my life should go. Sometimes life would move that direction, other times God had another plan. Needless to say, His plan always prevailed, even if I was kicking and screaming! I have always tried to do what I felt was right, what I felt God wanted me to do, even if I didn't agree. Sometimes His message was gentle; other times it hit like a bolt of lightning. This is one of those latter times! But this is, by far, the most heart-piercing plan I have ever been asked to walk through.

I know in my heart losing Ryan was part of God's plan. I know that because of the dream I had. I constantly remind myself of that, as it's the only glimmer of sanity I can find in my otherwise shattered life. I cannot understand why God would take my baby from me at such a young age. Why my Ryan? Why does He want me to walk this unbearable, painful journey? Why has He chosen me? How do I survive this and ever feel joy in my heart again? His plan has broken me.

The battle rages in my heart. I know there is a reason, and I also know we are told not to question His will. But when your child is taken from your arms, you WILL question. Not only do you question, you want answers! Despite these feelings, I question with an open heart. I am desperate for answers, and open to any good, any blessing, that can come from the death of my young boy. God's will was not mine this time — and this is the most painful, demanding, and seemingly impossible thing God has ever asked of me. Again, I ask: why has He chosen me?

Blog Entry:

Wednesday, October 27, 2010

Memories and Emptiness

Today has been very hard. When I stop and allow myself to feel, it is almost overwhelming. It seems it would be easier to always surround myself with

people to distract me, but I know I need to be with the intense loneliness I feel as well. It is a very isolated, lonely, and frightening place to be. People tell me to think of the good times, the happy memories, and that will help me. I understand the idea of that, but it's not always the reality. Right now, in this moment in time, those very memories that brought so much joy to my heart, bring nothing but emptiness and tears. I miss Ryan and there is nothing that makes that better, nothing that lightens the heartache I feel. I miss my everyday interactions with my little boy: the hugs, the talks, the laughter, him asking me to cut his hair all the time, asking when dinner is ready, asking for a ride somewhere, his friends coming over as they all ate the night away, his honesty in sharing things with me, his genuine concern if he saw me cry, his need to somehow make my tears turn into laughter again, his footsteps down the hall each night as he came to wash his face, the way he would so freely tell me he loved me, the way he would smile when I told him, his playfulness, his perfectionist side, his carefree attitude, his ever growing confidence in himself, watching him ride his bike down the street as he headed to friends, his sweet voice, and his beautiful face, with big blue eyes, that I love so much.

One day all these memories may bring joy again, but for now, all they bring are emptiness, tears, and a gut-wrenching need to have my Ryan home with me again.

Blog Entry:

Friday, October 29, 2010

Frozen In Time

It's been just over a month since I lost Ryan, and although life has moved forward for others, I feel frozen in time. When you lose someone you love, you usually pause in time to grieve, but eventually you join the world again in moving forward. When your child dies, time freezes; and when the big world, your family and friends all start moving forward again, somehow you are not a part of it anymore. You just don't feel like you belong or feel you are a part of what you once were. Unfortunately,

34

I have experienced the loss of many people I love dearly, but never have I experienced a loss like this. Your child is a part of you, someone you gave life to, loved unconditionally; so when he or she leaves, a very large part of you goes with him or her. Your heart and soul are forever changed. You don't know who you are, what it all means, or where you go from here.

The only place I feel safe and comfortable right now is within my home. Perhaps because Ryan lived, loved, and laughed here. Perhaps because he died within these walls, in the room Russ built just for him. Perhaps because his ashes are on my dresser, surrounded by pictures, gifts he made and wrote for me, and his baby book. Perhaps because I am simply not ready — or able — to face the world again without him.

I don't know when I will be ready. I only hope and trust when the time comes, I will know the time is here. I am listening to my heart and following my instincts, trying so hard to take care of myself in this brokenness. If ever I needed to take care of myself, now is the time. I am still in shock and disbelief. I just can't believe this is happening most of the time. Maybe shock is God's way of protecting my heart from the unbearable pain, of this devastating reality. Maybe I am not ready to fully face that pain yet. I don't know. Little pieces of this reality are all I can take at a time. I do know that. I also know, for now, all I can do is try to get through each day, write in this blog to help me explore and release my heart's feelings, and continue to talk to Ryan, asking him to help me all the while watching the world go on without me — as I stand frozen in time.

Monday, November 1, 2010

Perpetual Sadness

The words of a beautiful song keep playing through my mind today: "When I am down, and oh, my soul so weary. When troubles come, and my heart burdened be. Then I am still and wait here in the silence. Til you come and sit awhile with me. You raise me up, so I can stand on mountains. You raise me up to walk on stormy seas. I am strong when I am on your shoulders. You raise me up to more than I can be."

I am trying to give myself hope that I will be lifted up, feel like more than I can be. In reality, I am still waiting in the silence. It's Ryan I want to come and sit with me, and the reality of him being gone leads to perpetual sadness within.

When I go to bed at night, he is all that fills my heart. I lay there, sometimes for hours, thinking about him and wondering if I'll hear him walk down the hallway. When I awaken, the first thing I think about is Ryan, wondering if I will ever wake from this nightmare.

Throughout the day, Ryan is always with me. In those moments when I feel brave enough, I let just a little bit of the reality that he's gone into my heart, and in that moment, I am instantly flooded with tears of anguish. To protect myself, I put walls up immediately. I can only take this in very small amounts at a time. This is all I can endure.

God took my baby, He knew how deeply I loved Ryan, the pain this would cause. He took him anyway. I will never understand the reason. I hope one day I can make something good come out of this tragedy, but never will I understand why.

I look at myself...the fairly serious health issues I have, and I wonder: why didn't God take me? I'm 50 and at least I have had a chance to live. I have lived

36

long enough to have dreams and the experience of chasing after them. I have felt complete joy and gut-wrenching heartache. I have lived.

Ryan was only 16, and his life was just beginning. He was a few weeks shy of getting his driver's license, something he was so excited about. He will never go to a prom. He will never celebrate his high school graduation. He will never skydive. He will never go to college and pursue whatever he dreamt of becoming. He will never graduate from college and know the indescribable feeling of "I DID IT!" He will never travel to other countries. He will never experience the complete happiness of looking into someone's eyes and saying, "I do." He will never have children to love the way he was loved as a child. He will never feel the joy of seeing his mom hold his child for the very first time.

Is a mother ever supposed to accept or understand this? If so, how?

I know I should focus on what he did do, and perhaps one day I will. God knows he did more good, understood more about real love in his short 16 years, than many adults ever accomplish or understand in their lives. He knew what loving meant, how God says it should be, and he lived it. I am extremely proud of him, and so incredibly grateful that God gave Ryan to me. He allowed me to be the mother who would love Ryan like no other could. That I was chosen to love and nurture this unbelievably special child was one of God's greatest gifts to me. But at this moment in time, my heart aches to hold him again, to hear his voice, to see his smile, and for all he will never experience in this life. And in my perpetual sadness all I can ask is: why my Ryan? Why?

Wednesday, December 1, 2010

Blessings of Ryan

Ryan has been a blessing to me from the moment he was conceived. Throughout my pregnancy, I knew the child within me was a gift, one for which I was ever so grateful, a gift given to me from God and taken away too soon by the very One who gave him to me. As I try to make sense of this, or at least find a little sense of peace, I am reminded of the blessings Ryan brought into my life, as well as to the lives of all who loved him.

Ryan was always a gentle spirit. His heart was tender and giving from the moment he knew how to share it. He did not like conflict with anyone, and he withdrew at its very presence. As he got older, when conflict surrounded him, he tried to calm the waters. If he couldn't find the peace he desired, he walked away from the situation. He believed in peace between people, in unity. He believed in reaching out to all he knew and loved, as well as reaching out to those he had never met before. He believed we should all love each other unconditionally, and he did not believe in passing judgment on others. He knew that was not his job or the job of any other person. He lived what he believed and knew to be right. At his young age, he KNEW what loving another person really meant. He understood what God meant when He said to love each other. Even at such a young age, he really understood.

With Ryan's death, I am left so empty. Yet I am also amazed at the power one young life has had on hundreds of people. As I think of him, I wonder if perhaps his early death wasn't some sort of sacrifice on his part, some understanding he had with God to better the hearts and souls of those he loved and who loved him. Perhaps if he were still here, we wouldn't be hearing and seeing the message of love we are all receiving now. This does not take away

38

*the ache in my heart, but it does help me see that
God has a plan, even if His plan has left me broken.*

*I pray that all who loved Ryan will keep their hearts
and eyes open, so that they will always listen and
see: Listen to the message of love he showed us in
his short life, and always See the blessings of Ryan.*

Blog Entry:

Tuesday, November 16, 2010

My Letter To Ryan

My Dear Ryan,

*It is almost 2 months since you left, and the aching
inside has no mercy. I look at your pictures around
the house — sometimes I touch your face,
sometimes I cry, and sometimes I just wish I could
hold you one more time. But I know one more time
would not be enough. To hear your voice, touch
your hair, and feel the joy I always felt when you sent
a smile my way — these are things I constantly long
for.*

*The house feels so empty now. You were such a
large part of my life, of my world, of this family. I
know I am not the only one hurting; and for
everyone who was close to you, I feel the emptiness
that has become a powerful reality in my life.*

*I want you to know, although I'm sure you do, that
your friends and I are looking out for each other.
You had such a variety of friends, which speaks to
the kind of heart you had. They are all so loving and
giving, and you need to know how much they have
reached out to me. So many of them have told me
how much you loved me, a gift so great they will
never understand it. I only hope I am bringing them
an ounce of the peace and comfort they bring to me
each day.*

Your brothers and sisters are all broken. They seem to deal with this in their own ways, which I try to respect. Whether it be diving into their work, their own families, their friends, they are just trying to survive, much like myself that way. I think the gut-wrenching pain of you being gone is too much for any of them to endure, so they keep themselves busy, trying not to think, perhaps avoiding a reality they are not yet ready to accept? Again, I understand that, but it worries me, too. I ask you to look after each and every one of them; and when the time comes, and they fall down in pain, please help them stand up again. Let them know you are there and you believe in them. They will need that from you. Knowing you are with them is where they will find the strength within to get through this and continue on. They will never get over it, but they can get through it.

Ryan, please let them all know you are there.

Myself ... I'm sure you see what has happened to me. I know you never liked to see me cry, and I'm so sorry you have to see me broken like this. I actually feel guilty that you would see me in so much pain, but I'm sure that doesn't surprise you. You know how deeply I loved you, how close we were, how special you always were to me. So I'm sure you understand the anguish I'm feeling. I believe you are with me, and I thank you for always letting me see that. I ask you to continue to watch over me, too, because sometimes I don't know how I will get through this. I don't know who I am anymore, or who I am becoming. I know you always believed in me and the woman I was, so I will try and draw from that to pull myself up again. I would never want to let you down.

You ... I am happy you are with my dad again. I am happy he came to get you, and I know he is so proud of you. I am happy you feel a joy and love like no one here could begin to understand. You gave love so freely to others; you deserve the love you are living in now. Is it everything I told you it would be? I imagine it's so much more.

40

Even though my heart aches, I celebrate for you. I rejoice for you. I am so happy that you now know complete peace within. One day we will be together again, and you can show me all the beauty and love you have found in heaven. In that sweet moment when we meet, your Mom will touch your face, rub your hair, feel the complete joy of your smile, and hold you again in her arms like she always did — and has longed to do — every day since you left.

You are always in my heart Ry. I love you completely.

Mom

Blog Entry:

Monday, November 15, 2010

The Loneliness in Grief

Through the deep losses in my life, I have learned that grief is a very individualized process. Each person grieves differently, in his/her own time, in his/her own way. No way is right, no time is right, and no one can tell you how to do it. It is a road you ultimately walk alone, a journey you wish you never had to take but eventually will. Once that journey begins, there is no one who can wash away the pain. It is your pain, your journey, your grief.

Along the road you will meet many loving people who will try to help. Some with their words, their gifts, their genuine concern, their prayers, their love. Although this does not take away the hurt, it does allow you to know that you are loved; and we can never have enough love. Can we? There will also be some who say sorry, are present when the tragedy first strikes, and then quietly disappear into the night — perhaps because they don't know what to say, what to do, or how to help. I've never been one to disappear into the night, so I can't really understand or make sense of this reaction.

41

However, I do know there must be a reason, so I accept it as "their way."

When you lose someone, the reality is the only ones who will completely understand what you are feeling are the ones who have experienced the exact same loss. Whether it be the loss of an aunt, a grandparent, a parent or a child. It's almost as if you become a member of an elite club once you have experienced a loss, and only those club members understand what it's really about. Sadly, I have been a part of many elite clubs, but the loss of my son Ryan is the loneliest journey of grief I have ever been on.

When your child dies, no matter what the circumstance may be, a part of you dies with him. The child you brought into the world — to love, nurture, hold, protect — has been heartlessly ripped from your arms in the snap of a finger. It is a violent and physical separation. No mother should have to endure such pain. No mother should have her child taken from her. Nothing is the same. Your world is shattered to its very core. The woman you once were has disappeared, and you wait, wondering: what will the new woman be like when she finally emerges from the depths of darkness she is in? Will she emerge in one piece? Will she be able to love again, like she once did so freely? Will her family and friends know her? Will anyone recognize her?

Will everyone still be there, no matter how long it takes, waiting for her?

There is a lot of loneliness in grief; but losing my little boy, Ryan, is the loneliest journey of my life.

All of these blog entries capture the thoughts and emotions that ran through me following Ryan's death, all of which were my way of trying to understand what seemed impossible to grasp. I could not express the turmoil now the way I was able to capture it as it was happening. My entire world had collapsed. The foundation of who I was had been ripped from underneath my feet. It was all I could do to breathe. I didn't care if I lived or died. At times, the thought of death was the only thing that seemed to make any sense; the only thing that gave me peace. I couldn't work. I couldn't face people, and it seemed I had nothing left to say. I was completely empty inside. The world continued on, only I wasn't a part of it anymore. I didn't want to be. I had never felt so alone in my life. My mom, sister and brothers surrounded me, for which I am so grateful, but even they didn't understand the depths of my despair. How could they? I was alone in this. I could not make sense of what had happened. Why would such a good-hearted young man be taken at such a young age? Nothing in my life made sense anymore. The joy in my heart had been savagely ripped away and I had no reason to speak, sing, dance or even smile. I felt hollow, as if there was nothing within. The loving and happy heart I once had had not only been broken, it was shattered. How do you mend something that is now in a million pieces?

I couldn't remember how it felt to be happy. I could think back to happy times, but I couldn't remember how it felt. I remember thinking how crazy that was. How do you forget what complete happiness feels like? Something had turned numb inside of me and the only feeling I understood was pain. I was forever changed. Not understanding what that meant for me, I accepted it.

Besides myself, I witnessed the deterioration of my family. There were so many broken people, all with shattered hearts. Would any of us ever survive this? Would my family ever learn to be whole again? Was that even possible? What kind of family could we be with Ryan gone? How is a family ever complete when there is a person now missing? Would we ever feel joy or a reason to celebrate? Each person in my family was changed, which meant our family as a whole had changed. Our family was broken. Once more, I didn't know what this would mean for us, or where we would go from here, but I knew I needed to help them all. In this, I found a reason to move forward again.

Chapter 3

A Family Broken

Blog Entry:

Monday, November 21, 2010

The Pain of My Children

Tomorrow is the second month anniversary of Ryan's death. My heart is heavy today, not only for my own loss, but for my children who are still living, carrying the pain and emptiness of losing their brother.

Ryan was blessed to have many brothers and sisters. He was loved by all of them, and loved them in return. When he died, a part of them died as well. I know this is their journey to take, much like my own, but as a mother you can't help but feel their pain, suffering in the realization that this heartbreak is one you can't heal. Like myself, they each have a journey to take, and although we can support each other along the way, they will ultimately walk the road alone. How does a mother accept her child is hurting and she can't fix it? I know every mother asks this question, but when a child dies — a brother —the question cuts much deeper.

I have witnessed great sorrow with my kids. I have heard the painful cries of brothers and sisters when they heard the news that their brother died. I have seen the endless tears. I have felt the unexplainable anger spilling out of them as they yelled through their cries. I have seen their unforgettable anguish as they said their final goodbyes. I have helplessly listened to their cries: "I just need something to make me happy again." "Am I ever going to stop feeling so sad?" "I just want Ryan back. That's all I want." "I miss him so much. Is this really happening?" "I can't deal with this pain. I don't have anyone to talk to. I'm all alone." "I don't want to cry, so I hold it inside. I can't deal with this, so I try not to think about it. Why Ryan?" "I want to be with Ryan; I just want to die." Each cry has broken my heart a little more, yet I encourage the tears and desperate cries because I know they need to let these feelings out. I know they must walk through the pain to get to the other side, even when it feels like it will completely consume them. Yet with this knowledge, I also know the fear that can leave you paralyzed.

Why is my heart so heavy? Because I know they must all walk this painful journey, and I cannot walk it for them. No mother wants to see her child hurt. The instinct is to make things better again. For the first time in my life, there is nothing I can do to make any of this better. I am as helpless as my children. I am broken, too. For a moment I think I am failing

46

them somehow, but then I realize I am letting them see me in my brokenness, letting them see the woman I am, the mother I am. Is honestly sharing your heart with your child failing them? I don't think it is. At least I hope not.

What I can do is try to give them hope — hope that there will be a tomorrow, that Ryan will always be with us, and we will feel joy again. We will probably never get over this, but we will learn to rise from the ashes and live again. It will never be the same, but that doesn't mean there won't be happiness. For now, while hearts are still aching, I just pray that my kids know I am here, that they know I am always the safe place they can fall. That even though I am broken inside, I am never too broken to hold them in their pain. That I need them as much as they need me. That I am their mom, and although I am grieving the loss of one child, it does not mean my love for my other children is any less.

I love my kids, and because of this love, I will always carry their pain, no matter how much pain I am feeling myself. I hope their hearts know this to be true.

Without a doubt in my mind, the greatest heartache or devastation a parent could ever bear is the loss of a child. It is unimaginable and indescribable. That being said, we as parents carry many other heartaches with our children, one of which is seeing them stand in front of us in complete pain. All I wanted to do was ease their pain and find a way to heal their hearts. Unfortunately, this was a time in life when I couldn't make things better. It left me feeling helpless and useless.

When Ryan died, our entire family changed. Besides the devastation I was feeling so deep within, I knew my kids were feeling the same. All of their hearts were shattered. It was overwhelming to know there was nothing I could do to make things right again. How could I? There was nothing right about any of this. I remember thinking that I was 50 years old and couldn't wrap my mind around what had just happened, so how could my kids ever come to terms with it?

Everyone dealt with things differently. At the time of Ryan's death, there were three kids left at home, and three who were on their own. One child acted like nothing had happened and would only talk about Ryan when it was brought up to her. She wanted to go to school the next day; and I suppose it was to have a sense of normal, at least as much as she could control. My youngest was 4 at the time and talked about Ryan all the time. She cried often and asked many questions about heaven. She was very open with her feelings and the incredible loss she was feeling. Another child surrounded herself with friends for weeks and slept with me for many months to follow, asking me each night if she was going to die. Throughout the year she started developing different physical ailments, all of which I had checked out with doctors. She held so much inside; and I knew it had to be released somehow, so I was not surprised when she started having physical reactions. I knew counseling was needed, but I had to wait until she was ready. She was so afraid to deal with the hurt inside and I couldn't blame her. After all of the doctor appointments, she finally agreed to counseling. One of my older children completely fell apart. He was in college at the time, a time when your life is supposed to be exciting and carefree. His life turned upside down and he lost all passion and motivation for anything. He was sinking in a black hole and I didn't know how to pull him out. Depression became evident to me, and his coming home for visits often seemed to be the one thing that helped. I did all I could do to help him, but carried an incredible worry that he may not recover.

The two oldest kids are on their own with their own families. My daughter came over often during the first month, crying uncontrollable each time she walked through the door and saw me. We spent a lot of time talking and crying. The oldest carried much heartache but dealt with it in his own way.

I knew from my own past losses that each person grieves differently. With that knowledge, I respected and honored each child's process as they went through it. I did all I could do to help them in their grief. We would write notes on balloons the 22nd of each month and send them off to Ryan, which everyone really liked. I would listen to their words, yet paid extra attention to their silence. I helped financially when it was needed so my son didn't have another thing to worry about. At Christmas I got them Memory Blankets, each one with pictures of themselves and Ryan. I knew they needed a piece of Ryan and they all seemed so happy to receive these special blankets.

Being together seemed to help the most during the first few months. I did all I could do to try and lift them, yet I still felt helpless, worried and lost. I was unsure about everything and questioned if I would ever be able to be the mother they once had.

Sunday, November 7, 2010

Breanna's Letter To Ryan

My 4 year old, Breanna, has been coming to me over the past hour having me write notes on a piece of paper. It is a letter to Ryan, which she would like to mail to him. I wanted to be sure to capture her heart ...

"Sorry you died, Ryan. I just love you. I go to school and try not to miss you. You always loved me. I'm cute. I know you died, Ryan. Ryan loved Breanna and Annabel too. Ryan loved our family. The earth and the sun and the moon. Mommy is your family. Daddy is your family. Sean and Kaitie and Annabel and Breanna are your family. The cats are your family. Lucky is your family. Everybody loved Ryan. Everybody cried because Ryan died and went to heaven. I know you died. I really love you and really miss you. Eat healthy food. Mommy is the best mom for Ryan. Breanna is the best little girl. You always let me go in your bedroom and say hi to your friends. Because Mommy loved you, she always made you the best food ever. I very, very, very, love you so much. Because I love you I'm going to send a letter to you. Mommy is the best, best, mommy in the world. Because I love you, I want you to come back down. You can't come back down because you are in heaven. I'm going to send this up to heaven. I really want you to come down because I miss you and then I won't miss you anymore. I am sick. I am going to send this to Ryan. I'm going to make a rainbow. I like riding on a rainbow, too. I love riding on a unicorn. The end."

Spoken from the mouth of a babe, a babe with a very old soul. Breanna was so open with her pain, but not only that, she tried so hard at her young age to really understand what had happened. She needed to be able to accept it, and the way she did that was through writing and questioning. She asked me many times if Ryan could come back down and live here again. In her search for truth, we discussed heaven and all the possibilities that held. We talked about what a wonderful place it is and how one day we would all be there together again. She told me she hoped she died that night so she could be with Ryan again. I understood that longing for I had felt it myself. She wanted to know if Ryan could see us, and I assured her he could. She asked if he could hear us talk to him, and I promised her he heard every word we spoke to him. She wanted to know if he could talk to us or visit us. Although this veil had not been lifted for me yet, somehow I knew it was possible, so told her I thought he could. I told her he may visit in a dream or talk to her. She questioned whether we were still his family, and I explained we would always be his family. In her letter, which still makes me cry, I can clearly see her trying to process and understand the horrific loss this little 4-year-old had just endured.

Blog Entry:

Wednesday, November 3, 2010

The Pain of a Stepparent

As I walk through this painful journey, I seem to walk alone. Grief is a very lonely journey and one you ultimately take alone. You can have the support, love and prayers of your family and friends, but still you walk alone. Your heart is broken and no one can wash that pain away. You must walk through it and trust that you will survive, trust that God is beside you, probably carrying you, as you know there is no other reason you should still be standing.

As I begin this journey I am very aware of the pain around me, even though I don't know how to help Ryan's brothers and sisters, his dad, his stepparents, his grandparents, his aunts, his uncles, his cousins, and his friends. Today my heart is really consumed with the pain of the stepparent ... probably because it's Wednesday, the day his stepdad found him. Russ is always in complete anguish on Wednesdays, a pain I hope will ease for him with time.

Ryan was blessed to have a loving stepmom and stepdad. Ryan was almost 8 when they came into his life. I have always believed you can never have too much love! I know the loss of Ryan has brought much pain to both these people. I trust and hope Ryan's stepmom, Julie, is finding the comfort and support she needs to get through this. My husband, Russ, is having a very hard time, and I am not sure how to help him. I am not even sure how to help myself, so my inability to help Russ leaves me feeling useless.

Russ and Ryan were very close. Russ' nature is calm, laid back, and loving, which is exactly what Ryan is drawn to. Ryan never liked conflict; he was definitely a child of peace. Russ had a way of making Ryan smile and laugh when it seemed impossible for the rest of us. Every morning Russ would make Ryan his Hot Pocket, or whatever else he may have wanted, and deliver it to his room as he went in to wake him up for school. He would always tell Ryan he loved him, hug him, and even annoy him with a kiss now and again. Ryan knew the good in Russ' heart; he saw it in the way he treated me, the way he treats everyone. Russ also saw the love in Ryan's heart and never hesitated to let him know that, to let Ryan know how proud he was of him. For reasons unknown, Russ was chosen to find Ryan that painful morning of Sept. 22, 2010. I cannot imagine the shock, devastation, and anguish he felt as he called for help, called to tell me, and tried to help Ryan. The horror he must have felt as he watched the medics do their best to help my little boy. The feeling he has that somehow he did not protect my little boy for me. I have tried to assure him that is not how I feel, or the reality of what happened, but his heart will only accept that when it is ready.

Although my heart — the broken heart of a mother — is still in disbelief, anguish, and bewilderment, I felt I needed to express my concern, helplessness, and complete empathy for the pain of a stepparent. The stepparents should not be forgotten; and in my heart, they aren't.

Because I had divorced and remarried, my kids grew up with stepparents and stepsiblings. When I married the first time, I married a man with kids. I love those two very much, and I know there is great love between my kids and their stepparents. We all get along great and have traveled a long road together. During my grieving time and while witnessing my husband's relentless pain, I realized how much suffering they endured and felt it needed to be acknowledged. I suppose it was a sense of needing to reach out and let them know their grief mattered to me as well.

Blog Entry:

Saturday, November 6, 2010

One Life Ends and Another Begins

My oldest daughter, Shawndre', just found out this week she is expecting her second child. After over a year of trying, for some reason, God felt now was the time. She is not sure of the due date but had a test today which revealed she is at least 6 weeks pregnant, taking it back to around the time Ryan died. She has been telling me she needed

53

something happy, something to look forward to, in order to get through this pain. It seems her prayers were answered; and perhaps her brother, Ryan, is looking after her. As we talked about this, my little girl cried. She really feels Ryan is with her now.

I am very happy for her and her growing family. I am happy for our entire family. We all need joy at this time in our lives. We need to see there is a morning light that will shine through, especially since the world seems so dark right now.

I feel so many different emotions with this new blessing: happiness, sadness, confusion, gratitude but, most of all, joy — joy for what Shawndre' is feeling in her heart. I feel I am witnessing the circle of life. God has taken a life from our family; He has given a life back to us. This does not wash away an ounce of the grief I feel or lessen my intense longing to have my Ryan home with me again, but I know it has given Shawndre' something to rejoice in. For that I am so grateful. It's one of my children that I feel will somehow be OK now. She needed something good and happy to help her through. She asked, and she was heard.

I have said before that I have always felt Ryan was my "miracle baby" due to the situation at his birth. I now feel, as does Shawndre' that she has been given a "miracle baby" and somehow Ryan feels very alive in this.

I believe this miracle baby gave Shawndre' the will to move forward. She had a new reason to move forward. She would come to my house, cry her heart out, and ask if she would ever be happy again. I completely understood and lived those very emotions. Shawndre' was so consumed in sadness, she saw no light. She said many times she just needed something to look forward to. She decorated her house for Christmas in October, thinking that might help. I believe it did for a small while but not for long.

54

By the way, she still decorates her house early each year. When Shawndre' found out she was pregnant, she was given the very gift she had asked for, something to look forward to. I was very happy for her as I knew her heart would be lifted somewhat as she focused on the pregnancy. I felt bad because I didn't feel the joy I normally felt when she was pregnant. I couldn't grasp, or even remember, what real joy felt like. I did the best I could do, and I genuinely celebrated the birth of her son, Jayden Ryan.

Blog Entry:

Friday, November 5, 2010

A Mother's Love

I have spent much time today thinking about love. In particular, the love a mother feels, and gives, to her child. I believe this is the greatest earthly love there is — the love that is most reflective of the love God asks of us and gives to us. A mother falls in love the moment she knows a child is within her womb. Every time you hear the heartbeat or feel your baby move, you fall deeper in love. Then the miracle of birth is given to you, an indescribable experience of pain and joy like no other. During the painful moments and hours of labor, the love you have for your unborn child is what gives you the strength to endure the physical pain. Already, you have an unconditional love and determination to do anything for your child, to endure anything that is asked of you.

When your baby is born, you hold in your arms what you consider to be a miracle. Instantly, you feel an overwhelming love, one like you have never known — a love so deep, you didn't even know it existed. Your child has become the center of your world, your love, your life. As your baby grows, your love grows. You nurture, protect, and love like you have never done before. These feelings, this love, fills every part of your being. As your child continues to grow, because of this mother's love, you are always able to see into his heart, even when you don't like something he is doing. You are able to move through any hurt to try and understand, because you know and believe in his heart. You see the good, and you never stop believing in that good, no matter what is going on. You continue to love, protect, nurture, defend, and feel extreme pride. You give him everything you have, selflessly, expecting nothing in return. And if you are blessed to have more than one child, you feel the exact same feelings for each child; the heart of a mother grows with each child.

This kind of love is pure and genuine. I believe it is given by God. I believe it is the strongest and purest of loves on this earth. Because of this, when a mother loses a child, the pain and loss are beyond words. Unless it has happened to you, it is completely beyond comprehension. Your child is your heart, your world. So when any one of them is taken, a big part of your heart and world go with him. The woman you once were is forever changed. You don't know who you are anymore. You are left empty, trying to make sense of it all, trying to pick up the pieces of your shattered world, when you barely have the strength to stand. Trying to figure out how you will survive the anguish, and how much strength you have to endure it. Trying to understand how you will ever find joy in the world again, when one that brought you so much joy is gone. Trying to make sure your other children are okay, and know that your love for them hasn't changed despite the fact your life has just been shattered and love has been ripped right out of your soul. You are left with your own pain and sorrow but also the need to take care of your other kids, even when you feel you have nothing left to give, even when you question your ability to love again.

I am praying and trusting that my mother's heart will guide me with regard to my other kids, so they continue to know how much they are loved — even by their mother's broken heart.

I found myself completely shattered as a woman and a mother. My children were in such despair, and I questioned by ability to help them when breathing seemed to be a challenge for me. Was I still capable of giving them the love I felt for them and the love they deserved? Did they even realize how much I still loved them?

I loved Ryan with every fiber of my being; and with his loss, I could not move. I felt frozen in time. I was in such turmoil within. I couldn't sleep, so I was walking around in exhaustion most of the time. Ryan was in my mind constantly. I found myself trying to remember every curve in his face, how his eyes sparkled, how deep his dimples indented when he smiled, the feel of his soft red hair, and the sound of his footsteps as he walked down the hall. I would have given my life at any given moment to hear him say "mom" or "I love you" one more time.

My pain was so deep at times that it literally scared me. I could only let myself go into that darkness for brief moments at a time. When I entered that empty place I would just want to die. I actually thought of ways I could die, which I did not want to admit to anyone, let alone myself. When I hit that place of complete darkness, I would quickly do something — anything — to get my mind on something else because it was so powerful and all-consuming, it truly frightened me.

I remember I had a mass in my sinuses and was scheduled for surgery before Ryan died. Two months after he died I had the surgery. I didn't care if it was cancer, for I already knew there was nothing I couldn't handle. I knew there was no greater pain in this life I could ever feel after losing Ryan; not even losing my own life scared me.

As I tried to deal with my own grief and the piercing pain of watching my kids suffer, I was witnessing my husband, Russ, deteriorating. He is the one who found Ryan the morning he died. Not only was Russ dealing with grief of losing him, he was dealing with the trauma of what he had witnessed. He was also carrying the burden of feeling that in some way he hadn't protected my son for me. As much as I tried to assure him it was out of his control and in no way did I find him at fault, he couldn't let it go.

Russ began to do what many choose to do when they can't deal with the pain facing them; he turned to alcohol. At first I completely understood his need to numb his pain. I knew it was a traumatic event and probably too much to deal with at the time. I accepted the drinking. I assumed it was a temporary crutch he would use until he felt strong enough to cope with the reality of what had happened. What started out as a numbing effect turned into a way of life.

As months went by, the drinking did not stop. As time passed, I began to question the drinking, at which time he tried to hide it. I would call him out on his secretive drinking, and he would deny it. With the hiding came lies; with lies came fighting. He was dealing with anger in his grief process, which did not blend with alcohol very well. Before I knew it, our relationship was unraveling at an incredible speed. I would try to talk to him, but catching him sober was becoming a rare occurrence, so the talking did not help. I began to feel very angry and resentful. My son had just died, my children were in desperate need of help, and here was my husband living in a state of drunkenness. How could he abandon me when I needed him the most? How was I supposed to help my kids, deal with my own growing pain and also help him? I realized this was a problem that had gone beyond the original need to numb. I was ready to snap, and I knew I couldn't let that happen.

I finally decided I needed to take a leap of faith. It was my only chance to help Russ and save our marriage. I knew it was a gamble because I didn't know how he would respond. However, I knew if I allowed things to stay the way they were, the poison of our relationship would further damage our kids, and I was not willing to take that chance. I couldn't deal with any more than I already had. I felt I was about to lose my mind and everything left in the world that mattered was about to be destroyed.

I told Russ that he needed to get himself into rehabilitation before the school year was out, or he needed to move out. This gave him three weeks to decide what he wanted to do or was capable of doing. I had been given the name of a rehab facility by a friend, so I handed it to Russ. When school ended, Russ had arranged to go into a rehab program the following Monday. I was so grateful and relieved. I drove him there on his scheduled admittance day, and I made sure I visited him every weekend so he knew I was supporting him. He was gone for a month and came out the man I had known before. Additionally, he was ready to face his grief without substance to numb it. I was able to deal with my own pain with his support. I am grateful that his love for me, Ryan, and our family was more important than his need for alcohol. He showed great courage and strength, and continues to do so. I learned clearly that sometimes you have to take that leap of faith, a lesson I would continue to remember as spiritual doors began to open.

Blog Entry:

Friday, August 9, 2013

The Survival of a Marriage

Walking along the beach this evening, Russ and I talked about how we have grown even stronger since the loss of Ryan. For that, we are both grateful.

When together you lose a child, your relationship is immediately put on the list of "at risk marriages." We didn't know that when it happened, and it was honestly the last thing on our minds, but time surely showed us we were at risk! When this type of devastation and loss strikes, you are both taken into depths of darkness you didn't know existed. Each person carries his/her own pain yet also bears the pain of the partner. You don't know how to make it better for the other, and you absolutely don't know how to make it better for yourself. How can you possibly make something better that is so painfully wrong? It's a very lonely journey, and I can easily see now how many marriages don't survive the loss of a child.

When Ryan died, we both felt pain that words could never describe. Russ was the one who found Ryan, so he carried guilt and a profound feeling that he should have been able to do something. In his eyes, he was entrusted with the care of my baby, and he felt he somehow let me down. Although I did not feel that way, it was his pain and the journey on which he would embark. As much as I tried to help him understand it was not his fault, he could not let that go. That all-consuming pain led him down a very dark, angry, and isolated road — a road of self-destruction. Meanwhile, I was trying to help him while also helping my kids. I felt very alone, yet knew I had to find a way to lead them all through the darkness. I was on a road I had never traveled, didn't want to be on, and I had no light to guide me; there was only darkness.

I listened to my heart and desperately tried everything I could to help make things right somehow. I was walking alone; Russ was walking alone. Somehow we had lost each other in the unbearable pain of it all. My own grief had to be put aside, as I watched my family falling apart. At that time, I didn't know if Russ and I would make it. There were times I didn't care, and I'm certain he felt the same. I couldn't bear any more pain; I knew that. I also knew that as a mom, I had to be sure my kids made it. They quickly became my focus. As moms always do, I put my own pain on a back shelf. In retrospect, perhaps the needs of my family helped me survive that first year.

Nine months after Ryan died, our marriage hit a crucial point. Russ and I couldn't be further apart, and after 30-plus years of friendship, that just brought more sadness upon hearts that were already broken. It was then Russ stood up, faced his demons, and did all he could to make himself all right. He did it for me. He did it for our kids. He did it for Ryan. He taught us all about courage and respect, showing strength I had never seen in him before. His actions at that time clearly told me how *strong his love for me was, and I met him with encouragement, compassion and gratitude.*

It's been almost 3 years now. We each carry the pain and loss of losing Ryan deep within our hearts. We are learning to share that grief, when we are able. We are able to see the silent pain and respect that place in each other. The darkness born from the loss is still deep in both of us, but we have learned to face it together. When the pain is so deep, I can't talk, and isolating my heart is the only way I can endure any given moment. He shows me he is there, if and when I'm ready to share.

We have been given challenges and pain most couples will never endure. It was a very painful road as a couple for almost a year, but our love, friendship, loyalty and determination helped mend what was broken. I am so very grateful that we have the type of relationship and marriage that has survived the deepest of heartbreaks — the death of a child.

Chapter 4

Nurturing My Heart

Blog Entry:

Wednesday, November 24, 2010

The Comfort of the Ocean

We all need a place to run, a place where we feel safe from the hurts of the world, a safe place to fall. The ocean has always been a place of peace, spiritual growth and comfort, a place where God always holds me. If ever I needed to be held by God, it's now.

I was blessed to have had a couple of days there, thanks to the generosity of my brother. As soon as I saw the raging sea, my chest opened up, and for the first time since Ryan died, I felt like I could breathe again. I knew I needed to be there, and I'm sure God knew it as well.

For my entire adult life, I have run to the ocean when I was in need, when I felt turmoil inside, when I needed peace, when I wanted to feel close to God. Watching the majestic waves always makes me feel the power and wonder of God, helping me remember He is in control. Although I don't always understand the reasons for things, I am able to somehow let go a little and trust things will be OK. Perhaps this is the peace that seeps into my heart when I stand before the ocean watching waves crash against the rocks and cliffs. As I watch the waves roll in and out, and I am reminded of change, of life constantly moving, of love coming and going, and coming again, of pain and joy. I am reminded that nothing stays the same, no matter how much we wish it could. Yet, I am also reminded of how things do stay the same.

This is the first time I have ventured out since Ryan died. I went where God was calling me, where He always calls me. I wrote notes to Ryan in the sand. I looked for hearts in the sky. I talked to Ryan. I talked to God. I cried. I sang "Testify to Love" over and over as I walked along the beach, tears streaming down my face. In doing these things, I was reminded I need to nurture my heart, because it is broken and needs the tenderness and comfort only God can give. The ocean is the one place I surrender and really allow God to hold me in my brokenness. As I returned home, the anxiety and fear began to build, the tears began to fall, and I knew I must return soon. I will return to the ocean where I will allow God to hold me again. I will feel Ryan with me, and I hope each time I go I can build a little more strength within to continue to endure and move forward. The comfort of the ocean for me is, in fact, the comfort of God.

Blog Entry:

Sunday, December 5, 2010

Searching For Peace

Sometimes the turmoil inside is so strong, so overpowering; it seems as if there will never be a sense of peace again. I am not expecting to find complete peace or acceptance — I know they will never be mine. I don't imagine after losing a child you ever feel complete peace again. After all, your child is no longer with you. However, a sense of peace is needed to move forward and allow you to breathe. At least it is for me.

My greatest peace comes from the ocean. It is there I find some sort of comfort in this insanity, a small sense of peace, letting God's love and majesty completely surround and fill me. Those visits are not nearly as often as I need them to be, but they do help while I'm there. I have been reading a lot again, searching for that sense of peace my heart desperately needs right now — books about faith, afterlife, near death experiences, the paths of other people who have lost their children, etc. I am so open to everyone's ideas, thoughts, and feelings, passing no judgment on the journeys they are on.

I know how hard life can be and how much we all need peace in our hearts. When you lose a child, you are thrown into a very lonely, quiet, and seemingly impossible place. It takes every bit of strength to get out of bed each day and try to resume a semi-normal life for the rest of your family. All the while, nothing feels normal within yourself. I don't even know what normal is anymore. I don't know how I am supposed to function in the world as I did before. I don't know when this overwhelming feeling of sadness will ever lighten. I don't know when I will feel joy in my heart again, or if I ever will. Nothing is the same; nothing feels right. I am a mother who has lost her child. Even now, I cannot seem to wrap my head around that reality.

65

I continue getting up each day. Sometimes I feel like I'm numbly walking through the day, other times I know I am barely crawling. I continue trying to meet the needs of my family, although I'm sure I fail them in many ways. While I go through the motions, deep in my heart I am fighting and frantically searching for some sense of peace.

Blog Entry:

Thursday, August 8, 2013

The Confusion Within

Once again, I have come to my place of peace — the ocean. Since Ryan died, it is the one place I actually feel at peace within. It's my time to reflect, to try and understand, to question, to cry, to remember, to wonder, to nurture myself, to just be.

Today as we were driving along the coast, I felt very quiet. I was frustrated at the delays we faced in getting to the place I so needed to be. In those frustrations, I once again started looking at the woman I have become since I lost Ryan. In my thoughts, I realized how confused I am about so many things.

One moment I think I need to hold onto my other kids tightly, protecting them, because I never know what could happen to them. In the next moment, my heart tells me to let go. After all, Ryan died while sleeping in the safety of his bed. I couldn't protect him in the safest place possible; what makes me think I could protect anyone else? One moment I think I need to really be sure to appreciate each moment in life because I've been painfully shown how short and unpredictable life can be. In the next moment, my heart tells me that can never fully happen again, because I don't feel the joy or passion in life the way I use to. One moment I think I need to find a way to make something special out of my life, to find new dreams. The next moment, my heart remembers all the dreams that were shattered, and I wonder how much longer I'll have to wait before I get to see — and be — with my Ryan again? For everything I think or do, there is an opposite feeling or reaction happening.

The very day Ryan died, I knew I would never be the same woman I was before. I knew I had changed. I didn't understand what it meant, but I knew it was my new reality. It's been almost three years, and I still see the changes happening. I'm still not sure of who I am, where I am meant to be, or why all of this even happened. This grief has no answers, no clarity, no end. I am still very saddened and bewildered — yet accepting — of the confusion within, the confusion of Me.

After Ryan died, I wouldn't leave the house. I didn't want to see anyone or speak to anyone. I was literally afraid of the world that had gone on without me. After Ryan's death, my brother offered immediately to send me to the coast because he knew how healing that was for me. I could not even bring myself to go there, even though my heart told me that was exactly what I needed to do. About two months later I knew I needed to be alone and find some sort of inner peace. It was time to go to the ocean. That was the beginning of the spiritual journey I was to embark upon.

When I saw the ocean, I physically felt a weight lift off my chest, and I felt like I could breathe for the first time since Ryan died. I was able to just "be" without worrying about taking care of someone else. I cried, talked with Ryan, sang to him, talked to God and cried endless tears. In all of this, I felt comforted and free inside to be who I needed to be and feel what I needed to feel. It was such a gift and I knew immediately it would be my Place of Peace. I began my blog there in my retreat and completed most of the blog writing there. It is also where I began my book, and as I type now, I am sitting at my Place of Peace. It has become a place of healing, creativity and spiritual awakening.

Blog Entry:

Thursday, September 26, 2013

The Gift of Friends

I am at my "Place of Peace" trying to find some healing after the anniversary of Ryan's Death. It is the one place I feel like I can really breathe. The wind is fierce tonight, which creates powerful waves — exactly what I need. The sound is healing to my soul, and I am so grateful for this time here.

Tonight I was fortunate enough to be able to spend some time with a very close friend of mine and her incredibly sweet husband. They happened to be here at the same time I was coming. My time here is usually spent alone, for many reasons, but sharing my special time and place with someone so close to my heart seemed so very right. I am so grateful we did it!

On this journey I have been forced to take, there is little that really brings me comfort. Nothing seems to be able to take away the pain or ease the brokenness within. But there are things which help me endure the loneliness along the way. A good friend is one of those things — someone who listens, and as she listens, with every sparkle in her eyes you can see the love and compassion shining from her soul; someone who cries with you, laughs with you, and somehow seems to feel your hurt even though you both know it's impossible; someone who is not afraid to speak your child's name and also seems to know how important it is for you to hear;

someone who also listens with genuine interest and unconditional love every time you speak his name; someone who always asks how you are doing, as well as the rest of your family, because she seems to know that even though time has passed, the pain has not; someone who encourages your every step and celebrates every small victory as you try to move forward; someone who gives you a safe place to fall; someone who loves you enough to really show it.

I am grateful for such friends in my life. I don't know if they even understand the importance they play in my life. Do they know how much they lift and carry me during my saddest moments? Do they understand how they gently bring light into my darkness? They may not know my pain or what it's like to lose a child, but they know me. They know my heart. They hear my words, and they understand my silence. They are my friends, and they are a gift in my life. They help me take One Small Step at a Time.

Blog Entry:

Saturday, October 30, 2010

Random Facts About Ryan

~ He was born on March 17, 1994 at 10:45 p.m.

~ The umbilical cord was wrapped around his neck twice, so they had to reach inside to cut it as he was in major distress. He was purple/blue when born and immediately given oxygen. I always felt he was my "Miracle Baby" — I still feel this way.

~ He was a quiet, peaceful baby.

~ He was a happy toddler, always smiling.

~ He used to call Kaitie, "My Kaitie baby."

~ He loved scrambled eggs for breakfast when he was small. Had to have them every day!

~ He always told me he would live with me forever.

~ He loved playing by himself when he was little.

~ He went camping for the first time at 3 months old.

~ My dad use to call him "the camper."

~ He always loved the outdoors.

~ One time driving over St. Helena Mountain, he stuck his head out the window and said, "Nature always makes me feel better."

~ His brother, Sean, was always his hero.

~ He loved all of his brothers and sisters.

~ He loved family vacations.

~ He loved to fly places in airplanes, but felt nervous, so he always carried his Bible on every trip we took.

~ He always loved going to Disneyland. We have taken many trips there. As he got older, he would take off with his older siblings while we were there, and he really loved that.

~ He loved his bed because I put two memory foam pads on it for him.

~ He loved his bedroom, and even helped Russ a bit in building it.

~ He fell in love with Hawaii when I took the kids in 2008. He always wanted to go back. We were planning to do that again next year.

~ He loved swimming with the dolphins in Hawaii.

~ He ate two pizza hot pockets every night before he went to bed. Sometimes he would add a ChimiChanga.

~ He ate a ham and cheese hot pocket for breakfast — loved it with a little orange juice.

~ He loved steak and baked potatoes.

~ He was very humble.

~ He was very intelligent.

~ He did not think he was anything special, just another person doing the best they could do.

~ He did not judge people; he accepted everyone for who he/she was.

~ He honestly loved all his friends unconditionally.

~ He was a "mama's boy" and proud of it. I was proud of it too.

~ He could not stand it if I was crying; it would often make him cry too.

~ He talked to me about everything, even the hard stuff.

~ He use to tell me, and I use to tell him, that he and I were alike in many ways and that's why we "got" each other.

~ His little sister, Breanna, could make him smile when he was in his worst moods.

~ He loved basketball. It was his passion, and he was gifted on the court.

~ He loved watching ESPN.

~ He played one year of football as a sophomore, and was moved to the varsity team during the year.

~ He loved watching the "Wizard of Oz." He never outgrew it and would always let me know when it was on.

~ He loved Christmas and the way the house looked and felt.

~ He loved the Christmas lights and outside decorations. He would always tell me if I needed to add something to make it better. Two years ago he said it was perfect. I have never changed it since.

~ He believed in God.

~ He highlighted passages in his Bible, all having to do with not judging others, not criticizing others, loving your enemies, and loving everyone the way we are told to love. He lived out each and every passage he highlighted.

~ He was carefree at times.

~ He was a perfectionist.

~ He would only let me cut his hair. He said I did it better than anyone at any place he could go.

~ His spirit was gentle, tender and giving.

~ His heart was open, generous, nurturing, accepting and completely loving.

~ He knew how proud I was of him.

~ He was my baby, my little boy, my Ryan, and he knew how much I loved him.

I have never been someone who took the time to nurture myself. In my life, everyone else always came first. I don't regret that, nor would I change that about myself, but what I have learned is I need to also take care of myself. When Ryan died, I was taken down to the ground. I felt as if everything in my heart and soul had been ripped from me, and I was left an empty shell. It was like I had to get to the lowest point possible in life, because only then would I allow anyone to help me. Only then would I allow myself to really care for myself. I quickly learned, out of a feeling of desperation and defeat, that I needed to nurture my heart or I surely wouldn't survive this.

Nurturing yourself can mean going to a certain place you feel peace, like the ocean. It can mean spending time with a close friend, someone who fills your soul. It can be sitting down and writing random facts about your child. Those random facts help to capture all of the small memories about your child, which now mean so very much. I found what nurtured my heart and soul, and I did it often. As time went on, I found myself doing it more and more. Each time I took the time to nurture my heart, my heart became a little stronger. Sadly, nurturing yourself can also mean separating yourself from certain people in your life.

When I lost Ryan, I needed the support of the people I loved. I am grateful for those people, and I will never forget the way they have helped carry me. A woman who had lost her son a year or so before me warned me that some of the people I would expect to be there wouldn't be. She also said that those you wouldn't expect would show up. I was amazed at how true these words were. It was hurtful at times, as she warned me it would be, because you want those close to you to show they care. I needed to know my son mattered, that my family mattered. I learned to let the hurt go because it had a way of eating at my soul. Again, I had to nurture my heart. Whether they didn't know what to say or didn't feel comfortable, it didn't matter. The end result was the same. I tried to accept their unknown reasons, but it still caused hurt and anger. Somehow I saw this as my son not being of importance, and I was not going to tolerate that in any way, shape or form.

I found the only way to nurture my spirit was to put distance between me and the people who didn't show they cared. I could not afford to carry any more hurt than what I was already carrying. I knew it would destroy me. I was not cruel or rude; I simply kept a distance. I knew that my heart, and the heart of my family, was the most important thing at this point. I had to do what was best for all of us. In doing this, I learned how important it was to surround myself with people who were able to show they cared and talked about my son without hesitation. This is what nurtured my heart. It is what I needed, and this is the path I chose to take.

I also learned what I was and was not able to handle. I used to feel guilty if I felt I was letting someone down. I had to shed myself of that mentality or I would sink deeper in the sadness which consumed me. If a large family gathering caused anxiety for me or my family, I opted out. If I was invited to some sort of celebration or event and I felt any hesitation, I listened to my instincts and didn't go.

I learned very soon after Ryan's death to listen to what my instincts — my soul — was telling me. Each time I did this, I had no regrets. When I did something I felt I was not ready to do, I regretted it. I did that a few times and learned very quickly that I couldn't afford to do it anymore. At first, I worried about what others would think. However, I soon came to accept the fact that if they did not ask or try to understand my reasons, they were not worth worrying about.

If people have judged me or gossiped about why I chose not to do something, then they are people who are not good for my heart and soul. The people who know me and have genuine concern always supported choices I made during that first couple of years, without question. Those are the people with whom I learned to surround myself.

Those are the people who have steadied me when I didn't feel I could stand alone. Those are people who helped nurture my heart and continue to do so.

Nurturing my heart was new for me but soon became a crucial step in learning to take one small step at a time.

Chapter 5

One Small Step at a Time

Blog Entry:

Monday, October 25, 2010

One Month Later

October 22, 2010, marked the one month anniversary of Ryan's death. Anxiety and sadness were building as the day quickly approached. Where had the month gone? Why did I still feel in shock after all this time? Was I ever going to be OK again? I wondered how I was supposed to feel that day.

I knew I needed to somehow pay respect to Ryan, to let him see us all pouring our love out to him. Yet I wanted to do it in a way that would be healing for his brothers and sisters. I then thought of balloons. Russ went out that morning and bought two heart-shaped, glittery balloons, with the words "I LOVE YOU" written on them. I decided we would all write notes to Ryan and then send them off to heaven.

The little kids were very excited when I told them;
they were sending Ryan a present. The older kids
understood the symbolism and were just as excited.
Sean, Bianca, Shawndre, Jay, Kaitie, Annabel,
Breanna, Julian, Crissy, Danny, Russ, and I all wrote
notes to Ryan on the balloons. Some tears were
shed as they wrote, some smiles. We went outside
around 8:30 p.m. with balloons in hand. Doing it
when it was dark was probably better as it would not
have been good if a balloon popped or was caught
in a tree! The moon gave just enough light for us to
watch them fly up, until darkness took them away.
We all gathered in our backyard, the younger kids all
holding on to the balloons with me, and at the count
of three we all let go and sent them to heaven. We
all watched, with squinting eyes, to see them as long
as we could. I said at one point, "I can't see them
anymore," at which time my 4-year-old said, "Maybe
Jesus caught them for Ryan." She took my breath
away, and when I caught it again, I assured her that
Jesus probably did catch them.

Blog Entry:

Thursday, November 25, 2010

The First Thanksgiving

I know Thanksgiving is a time to be thankful for all
we have, and I usually am. However, this year I had
a huge hole in my heart, a very loved son was
missing from the table. Being thankful for anything
was something I did with effort, not ease.

We went to my loving sister's house for dinner.
They offered to cook the Thanksgiving meal for us,
knowing how hard this holiday would be on us all.
For their sensitivity, love, and support, I am so
grateful. My mom, who is fighting a courageous
battle with cancer, was there. For the gift of her with
us for one more year of holidays, I am very grateful.
My children — four of them were with us — words
could never express the gratitude I feel for their

precious lives. Sean and Kaitie — I know they felt their brother's absence in a very painful way, and I share in that pain. The time together was very nice, although my heart felt so heavy. It was not until the end of the evening that the tears began to fall, when I was talking to my sister about turkey soup, something Ryan loved. My son, Sean, saw me crying and immediately held me. I know his heart was aching for Ryan, too. No matter how nice it was to all be together — and it was — it was not right without Ryan with us.

When we were leaving, my sister called me back to her front porch to look at something. On the cement step, out of what looked like dried mud sunken into the cement, was a perfect heart. Ryan needed us to know he WAS with us. Then when we started to drive home, a song played on the radio that I don't hear much anymore but have posted on my Facebook as a tribute to Ryan: "Testify to Love." Again, it was Ryan letting me know he was with us. I turned the volume up very loud and silently cried to myself so no one would know. I continued to cry the entire way home.

I am grateful that Ryan was with us. I am grateful that once again he let us know. I am grateful I, and those who love him, see the signs he continually sends. Although I always find comfort and peace in this, it wasn't enough this day. Today his spiritual presence did not comfort me like it usually does because today I wanted more. I wanted Ryan with me. I wanted him because it was Thanksgiving, because Ryan loved to eat, because Ryan is such a huge part of this family, because I love him so much, because he is my child. He is MY CHILD and was taken at too young of an age. For the first time since he died, I felt a glimpse of anger driving home, anger that all I have left are memories and signs of his spiritual presence, and not him here with us. I felt cheated out of a lifetime of loving him as we drove home, not only for me, but for my other children. I felt the unfairness of it all, and wondered "will I ever *be OK again?" Nothing is the same, and nothing feels right.*

I am always so grateful and comforted by the signs he sends; but today, on this first Thanksgiving; it just wasn't enough.

Blog Entry:

Saturday, December 11, 2010

As Christmas Approaches

Decorations are up, shopping is nearly done, and presents are under the tree. Despite all of this, my heart is painfully empty. As Christmas approaches, the sadness in my heart seems to grow stronger, which I didn't think was even possible at this point in my life. It is almost becoming too much to endure, which leaves me questioning my strength and ability to survive this journey I have been forced to take. I am filled with endless tears and an overwhelming anguish, an anguish I cannot even begin to describe.

Christmas has always been my favorite time of year. The birth of Jesus, the music, the decorations, the warmth of family, and most of all the love which people seem to give to each other so freely. I always thought it was sad that people didn't carry that love throughout the rest of the year, but at the same time I did feel grateful for the time it was here. What use to be my favorite time of year is proving now to be a time of devastating sadness and loss.

Ryan always loved Christmas, and so did his brothers and sisters. They love the decorations, the excitement of Santa, and the feeling of love that seems to be everywhere. If I had no other children, I would have crawled into my bed this year, hiding from the world. But I do have other kids, and because of that, I need to find a way to bring joy into their hearts. This Christmas will be hard on Ryan's brothers and sisters, so it's my job to do all I can to create a normal Christmas, all the while not knowing what normal is anymore.

I bought a small fiber optic tree and wrote Ryan's name at the base. I have placed two pictures of Ryan on each side of the tree. It is my way of paying tribute to him, and keeping him with us in a way everyone will notice. I know he will be in our hearts, but I feel there needs to be something special to look at, something which honors his life and his spirit with us. The fiber optic tree radiates like a rainbow, the symbol of hope God has always shown me in my darkest hours, the promise that things will be OK. I need that promise right now, so I brought it into my home and called it Ryan's tree.

I try to be excited for the kids, although I don't always succeed. I did everything I could to make the house look the way it always looked for Christmas, which took every bit of strength I had. I forced myself out into the world to buy gifts, even though I ended up breaking down during those shopping times. I am doing all I can to make Christmas right for my other kids, but deep within my heart I feel nothing but emptiness and sorrow as this first Christmas without Ryan approaches.

Blog Entry:

Tuesday, December 21, 2010

Three Months Later

As I write this blog, I am moving into the third month since I saw and spoke to Ryan for the last time on this earth. So many emotions are running through me, I don't know what to say. I only know I need to say something, because the sadness is building and must be released.

I don't know how grief is measured, or if it can be. I know there is no timeline, no right way, only my way. I don't know what "my way" is under these horrific *circumstances, so I continue to take it one day at a time. I have never been so shaken, thrown into such turmoil, or felt such heart-wrenching anguish in my entire life. There have been many times I have felt the ground beneath me ripped away; but in all those times, I have never felt completely broken like I do now. My world was shattered 3 months ago, and I can honestly say I am no better today than I was that fateful day of Sept. 22, 2010. I am still broken and am questioning when I will feel the pieces of my life are somehow coming together again — or if I ever will.*

After Ryan died, I managed to face what I had to do. I did what needed to be done, made the painful phone calls, worked with his dad in making decisions and arrangements, dressed him one last time before his brothers and sisters saw him and, finally, I poured my heart and soul into his memorial. It kept him close to me, and it was something I was doing in his honor, a gift to him. When the one month anniversary came, I arranged to write notes and release balloons with his siblings, a way to help them, while honoring Ryan. Then came Thanksgiving. I pushed through it, although inside I wanted nothing to do with it. Now Christmas is here, a time Ryan loved so much, and I have found the strength to push into this holiday as well, not for me, but for my family. I knew how important it was to make things as normal as possible, whatever normal means anymore. I am strong, I always have been. I do what I need to do, no matter how much sadness my heart carries. Because of this strength, I know I will continue to move forward, endure, and do whatever it is that needs to be done.

But underneath this strength is a woman who has a broken heart. A woman who will never get over this loss. A woman who will never stop missing her little boy. A woman who will always wish her son was still here. A woman who will forever long to see her son's smile, and hear his voice again. A woman who will always remember the joy Ryan brought into my life, into this family, and into the lives of so many.

82

Yet sadly, at the same time, I will think of all the things he will never get to experience. I am a woman who will never be the same person she was before, so perhaps I also grieve for the loss of me.

I am a strong woman, but I am also a broken woman. I am a woman who is a mother, a mother who lost her child, a child much too young to die. As I sit here with tears pouring down my face, I am certain of this: this pain is just as severe at 3 months as it was the day it happened. Perhaps it is worse now, because I am not protected by the physical and emotional responses that happen with shock. All I have now is the harsh reality, a reality I find very hard to accept and live with.

Blog Entry:

Thursday, December 30, 2010

The First Christmas

The first Christmas has come and gone; I survived. Did I feel the joy Christmas usually fills me with? No. Was there a painful void in the family gatherings? Yes. Will Christmas ever be what it once was? I doubt it.

My goal this Christmas was to make things as joyful as I could for my other kids. I knew they were hurting and felt the same anxiety about Christmas as I did. Somehow, I felt I needed to lead them through the holidays, even though I didn't know how I would survive them myself. I suppose that is the job of a mother, to stand strong and lead the way no matter how much you wish you could run and hide, no matter how much your heart is hurting or how unsure you are of which direction it is you need to move. As a mother, you must find a way. They needed me; their needs matter so much more than my own, and that is where I found my strength. It came from the love I have for my kids who are still here with me, as well as the love I have for Ryan. I

83

am certain that Ryan knew I would find my strength from this very love. I also know he was proud of my efforts, which matters more than I can say.

We had a very special time with the kids. We were all painfully feeling Ryan's absence, but together, we made it through. I got them all Vision Memory Blankets, which had pictures of each of them with Ryan on their individual blankets. I knew in my heart I needed to give them a piece of Ryan this year, so I spent hours putting these blankets together, and I addressed it to each of them from Ryan and me. They were all very touched, and I know the blankets meant the world to them. My instincts were right; they needed a piece of Ryan this Christmas. Throughout the evening we laughed some, we cried some, we talked of Ryan a lot. We brought him into this home with us, right where he belongs. And we missed him deeply.

We spent time with the Pyzers and Beebouts, as well as time on our own. Some family members shared their concern with words, a look, or a touch, gently letting me know they knew this was hard and they were there. Some spoke not a word, nor showed any signs of reaching out. To those who dared to address the sadness, no matter how uncomfortable it may have been for them, I am grateful. With their words and/or gestures, not only did they show me that my broken heart and the hearts of my husband and children mattered, they let me know Ryan was still a part of Christmas. I needed to know that. My entire family needed that. When my mom arrived, she walked in the door and handed me a small, artificial poinsettia to put under Ryan's tree. This was one of the greatest gifts I was given this Christmas. Some may ask, "What was the big deal with that?" Well, it was a very big deal to me. What it told me was she cared about my heart, she understood I was carrying an unspeakable sadness within, and she knew how important it was to bring Ryan into this Christmas somehow. She knew what Ryan's tree meant to me, so she added to it. What greater gift could anyone ever give a mother

84

grieving the loss of her child? I will keep that poinsettia forever, and each year when I put his tree out, that plant will sit under it, reminding me of the incredible gesture of love she gave to me, to Ryan, and my entire family that first Christmas.

Since Christmas, I have felt numb, shedding some tears at the most unexpected times, but for the most part, very numb. Perhaps this is a way to shield myself from the magnified sadness surrounding the holidays, perhaps a way to protect my heart from the pain I don't know how to deal with. Perhaps a way to survive the remainder of these dreaded holidays, perhaps a way to process how these first holidays were without Ryan here with us. Whatever the reason, I am almost grateful for the numbness. I'm sure it's part of the grieving process, and won't last for long; but immediately following this First Christmas, I welcome the numbness.

Blog Entry:

Sunday, January 2, 2011

A New Year Arrives

As New Year's Eve slipped in, I found myself feeling very reflective and confused. I had just experienced the most painful and devastating year of my life, so I would have thought I'd be grateful to see it end. However, it was also the last year that I had Ryan here with me to love, and be loved by. I didn't know how to face a new year without him. More than not knowing how was the fact that I didn't want to. He loved celebrating each new year, and that alone filled me with sadness.

I spent the evening alone, which in reflection, is exactly what I needed to do. It was an opportunity for me to gently sit with my heart and reflect on what Ryan has always meant to me — to honor the powerful and loving impact he has had on my life, and continues to have. It was a New Year's Eve I chose to spend with Ryan. I know he was here, right beside me. I sat down and watched the video from Ryan's memorial, crying the entire way through. I tend to hold my emotions inside, so I know the tears were meant to be shed. After watching the tribute to his life, I turned on home movies of Ryan when he was little. I watched my beautiful and quiet baby blossom into a loving and playful little boy. I remembered every detail, of every story, like it was yesterday. I remember how it felt to hold him, to sing to him, to play with him, to kiss him, to take care of him, to share in his laughter, to know exactly what he needed at any given moment, to always be the one who could make his world the way it was meant to be — the way he deserved it to be. As I watched, I witnessed the love we shared, the comfort we always found in each other, and the unbreakable connection we had right from the beginning of his life, all of which continued to strengthen and grow right until the day he died. I smiled, I laughed, and I cried. My son, at age 16, is dead. Seriously?

Soon after this I noticed it was snowing. My daughter, Kaitie, was at her dad's and very upset she was missing the snow. I told her perhaps it was a gift from Ryan, and I believed that. After I shared that with her, she was very insistent that I send her pictures. Not knowing if the snow would stick, I stayed up until 3 a.m. taking pictures for her. If Ryan was sending a gift, which she felt he was, I would be sure she saw it! The next morning, New Year's Day, our entire neighborhood was covered in snow. Snow, the pure and frozen rain from heaven. Snow is something which has always brought tremendous joy to my kids, something which I have always loved with a passion, something which radiates heavenly beauty in my eyes, something which has always lifted my soul, and filled my heart, something, which now, was making me cry.

A new year, a gift of snow sent from heaven — who could ask for more? I could, because when this this New Year arrived, NOTHING felt right without Ryan.

86

Blog Entry:

Sunday, January 16, 2011

My Return to Work

It has been almost 4 months since Ryan died, and I am now faced with the reality of my return to work. As they say, "Ready or Not." Well, I'm not.

The past months have been a blur to me. Although I remember exact details of the events which unfolded, the time is nothing but a painful blur. I don't know where the time has gone. Yet, at the same time, it has also been the longest 4 months of my life. I can't help but wonder if the rest of my life will play out in this slow motion, lifeless fashion.

I have spent endless hours reading and searching for answers and understanding so that my journey to acceptance will be easier. I have prayed like never before. Through this searching, my spirituality has grown stronger, and my eyes have been opened wider than I could have ever imagined ... but that's another blog! I have been the steady force in this house, even though I didn't know which direction to move most of the time. My husband and children have grown use to the security of my presence, although at times I'm sure that presence seemed worthless. I have had time to be with myself, I've learned to nurture my heart for the first time, I've been in prayerful meditation with Ryan and God, and I've been the listening ear and open arms when my husband, or one of my kids, fell crashing to the ground. Now I have to walk away from the safety of my home. I must return to the world I knew before Ryan died, a world which holds an entirely different place in my heart and life now.

When your child dies, you are paralyzed. Even though you go through the motions, to do only what has to be done, you are frozen within. I made it through the holidays, and I'm not sure how I did it. My heart wasn't in it, but I suppose the need to take care of my kids gave me the strength I needed to

87

face the storm. Life around me continued on; and for the first time, I was a spectator and did not even have the desire to participate. It took me 3 months to find the courage to walk into a grocery store. How could life move forward when my Ryan was gone? I still don't know the answer to that, but I know it does. Sometimes I feel angry watching people around me moving on with their lives as if nothing has happened. Then I remind myself that of course the life of others must go on. It is not their child; it is mine. I have tried to make sure the lives of my own children have gone on. In doing so, I make a point of keeping Ryan a part of our daily conversations, as well as a living force in this home. The older kids are keeping their lives moving forward, but it is clear to see they are also going through the motions. They are unsure of where their hearts have gone, if they will ever heal, and how they will REALLY feel joy again with Ryan gone. This loss is unimaginable, unspeakable, and has been completely devastating to each member of my family. Our journey has only just begun.

As for me, I am afraid to return to work. I am afraid to see faces of people I have not seen since Ryan died. I am afraid of what my students will say to me. I am afraid to walk into the classroom and look at my desk, the place I stood when I got the call telling me that Ryan was not breathing. I am afraid to be in the room where I felt complete and utter panic, fear, desperation and anger about being 40 minutes away from Ryan when he needed me NOW. I am so afraid of all those feelings rushing back to me and overwhelming me — like they are at this moment.

I am not ready emotionally, but I must return. I suppose I will just go through the motions until my heart catches up with me, whenever that may be. My priorities have changed, needless to say. I have changed. I still don't understand what that reality means; I just know it is. I know my well-being matters now, and I must continue to take care of me or I will be no good to anyone. I know my hurting family is at the top of my list, and I will keep them *there, without feeling guilty if it interferes with work. I always put them first, but would feel bad calling in sick. No more; they come first because that is the way it should be. That is the way it needs to be. They are what matters most, and right now, this entire family is walking around with shattered hearts. You never know what will trigger the tears or pain, but without a doubt, they are always triggered. My work has been extremely supportive, so I am hoping that comfort and support will continue upon my return, and for the months ahead. I'm sure it will.*

I guess I'm afraid because I don't know how to continue to take care of my heart, my family members' hearts, and return to work. The priorities are my husband, children (including Ryan) and myself. I will give all I am capable of giving to my job, whatever that may be. I just hope it's enough.

Blog Entry:

Saturday, January 22, 2011

Four Long Months

As I sit here, I find it hard to believe it has been 4 long months since I lost my son — 4 months since the world, as I knew it, was forever changed, 4 months since the life was ripped from my heart, leaving me breathless and broken. When I look back, the time is a mysterious blur. Perhaps the protection of shock? At the same time, the memories of what happened, and the exact details, are engraved in my mind with absolute clarity.

During the past months, my emotions have traveled on every realm possible. I have been in shock, in denial, in depression, in question of how I could have prevented this. But, the one feeling I have not owned, not yet anyway, is anger. Being someone who does not like conflict, I am certainly not missing the anger stage. The other stages of grief seem to come and go, fluctuating back and forth, with no rhyme or reason. They come as they will; and for the sake of my sanity, I have learned to accept the unpredictable process.

I have watched my children's pain and my husband's torment, and I carried my own consuming sorrow. None of us has any answers, but we manage to face each new day as it comes. My faith has been what I have leaned on, searched out and depended on to hold me up when I felt I didn't have the strength anymore to endure. Ryan has shown me numerous times that he is still with me, which has given me more promise, peace, and hope than I could ever explain. He has taught me so much about faith and spirituality, and I will always treasure his gifts to me. I thank him every day.

I recently returned to work. With the support of my coworker, and many other friends, I survived the first week back. We are completely cleaning and rearranging our classroom for a fresh start. That room is where I stood when the call came, telling me Ryan was not breathing. I stood in that room when my world came crashing in around me. I stood there while sheer panic permeated throughout my entire being. I knew the classroom would hold a lot of painful triggers, so with the advice of a close friend, I decided I needed to make changes in there immediately. Once the changes started, my friend (coworker) and I decided to clean the entire room. It may sound strange, but it has made walking into that room much more tolerable. It is hard enough to return to work. I knew I didn't need reminders and triggers of painful memories to haunt me as well. I also set up an area on my desk for Ryan. I have found that brings me comfort throughout the day. My heart is not with me at work, not yet anyway. For now, I am going through the motions. I have learned to do that very well over the past months. I am hoping that in time some of my heart and spirit will return with me as I head to work each day. Until then, I have accepted my return to work for what it is: a necessary step in taking care of my family. Without the support of my friends at work, I don't know if I would have made it through that first week. I will forever be grateful to all of them.

So many changes have happened in the past 4 months. I have been broken, I have felt the indescribable pain of losing a child, I have done what needed to be done to honor him, I have managed to get up each day (even when I didn't want to), I have somehow been there to love and support my family, I have faced those first holidays without Ryan, I have learned how to nurture my own heart and soul (taking numerous trips to the coast thanks to the support of my family), and I have recently returned to work, stepping back into the world that I don't feel a part of anymore.

Through all of this, I have survived. I am strong, and my faith is what carries me. Even with this faith, not a day goes by when I don't cry, when I don't feel overwhelmed by the pain of missing Ryan, when I don't wonder how I am supposed to live my life without him here, when I don't question if I even want to. As a mother, I carry many questions. Is Ryan happy? Is he OK? Does he have friends? Is he scared being there without me? Does he need me? I should have been there first to welcome him, to be his security and show him the glories of heaven. Is he doing all right on his own? No matter how strong I am, or how deep my faith, these motherly questions come frequently. After all, I am only human.

I am a mom who has lost her child far too soon. I am just trying each day to do the best I can do.

Blog Entry:

Wednesday, February 2, 2011

As Each Day Goes By

The days seem to continue on, as if nothing in life has changed. However, in my world, everything has

91

changed. I try to get through each day the best I can, one small step at a time.

I get up in the morning, and the first thing I think about is Ryan. I hit the snooze button and lay there in the dark, thinking and wondering. How am I supposed to survive this? How do I help my kids work through the fears and pain they carry in their hearts? When will the emptiness within be filled, or will it? Will my heart ever feel joy again? The reality of life, as I know it now, hits me right in the face with the dawn of each new day. As I drive to work, I am guaranteed to cry at any given moment and with no warning. I have learned to accept this; so when it hits, I let the tears flow. I try to put on the "I can do this" face as I begin the day. Again, at some point during the day, I am guaranteed to cry again. The days have become so long, and I find myself looking forward to the moment I can go to bed. The moment I lay in bed, I thank God that I made it through another day. I then pray with my entire heart and soul. I ask God to hold my kids in their pain, to keep them safe, to show me how to lead them through this, to hold my husband in his sorrow, to take care of Ryan for me and fill his heart with happiness, and to fill my soul with wisdom so that I may see and hear what this spiritual journey is teaching me.

I have found that some days I walk around in a thick cloud. I feel numb to everyone, and everything. These days are almost a relief, as the sadness does not forcefully permeate through me, reminding me of how wrong the world feels now. Then there are other days when I would give anything to feel numb. On these days, the sadness of what has happened is utterly overwhelming. My mind relives every painful detail, the anguish that no one could ever imagine fills me, and I find it myself filled with an indescribable sadness. I try to distract myself from these feelings as quickly as I can, because in all honesty, those moments are overwhelmingly frightening. Once more, when I lay in bed at night, I thank God I have survived another day, and the prayers begin.

I have learned to accept each day, each moment, as it comes. I know there is no manual or timetable to follow for grief, especially when you are grieving the loss of your child. Although I question my strength, my stamina and my ability to endure the rest of my life, I also acknowledge the fact that I am somehow surviving day by day. I am so grateful for this. With the Grace of God, the transcending love of Ryan, and the love and support of my family and friends, I am surviving as each day goes by.

Blog Entry:

Monday, February 14, 2011

The First Valentine's Day

I am amazed — yet not — at how hard the first Valentine's Day without Ryan was for me. I thought perhaps it might be difficult, since the day's focus is love, but I never dreamt it would take my breath away. I never imagined I would spend the entire day fighting tears — sometimes successful, sometimes not. Throughout the day, I reflected on past years. The knowledge of why this day was so hard became very clear.

I realized today that my feelings about Valentine's Day are very different from when I was younger. Prior to having kids, the "couple love" was Valentine's Day in my heart. Having that one special person who loves you. Once I had kids, what I consider the real meaning seemed to take on a whole new life of its own. I have always made it a priority to make sure Valentine's Day was special for my kids. I wanted them to know no matter what was happening in their lives, I would always be that "one special person" who loved them unconditionally. I didn't want them to think it was only about the love that a couple shares, but rather the love that friends share, a family shares, and a mother shares with her children. It felt important to me that they understand this day is about love, whether or not they anyone of them was in a relationship. A day to honor those you love, a day to honor love. More importantly, I wanted them to know how VERY MUCH they were loved by me. So in my typical fashion, I went out and bought little gifts for the kids, except Ryan. That is when I first realized this day would not be easy.

We celebrated Valentine's Day on Saturday, thinking that might make today easier for me. It didn't. I gave my kids their gifts, which they received in their usual excitement. The younger kids celebrated like it was Christmas, and the older kids understood what it all meant. In their wisdom and sweetness, I missed Ryan. I missed the way he would smile at me when I handed him his gift. As simple as the gift was, he knew how much love was behind it. He got it, appreciated it and, what really mattered the most to me, he KNEW how deeply I loved him.

Today I felt empty. I was in a classroom of excited students, and I felt no joy. I literally counted the minutes, knowing the day couldn't end fast enough. My mom stopped by at one point to drop off gifts for my kids. She told me she put a Valentine for Ryan next to a picture of him. A mother's heart is so loving, nurturing and thoughtful. It meant so much to me, that once again, she was keeping my little boy alive.

As the students passed out their treats and cards, I remembered how much Ryan enjoyed doing that when he was little. I remembered sitting with him and helping him address all of his cards. I remembered how I had to get cards with candy or stickers, because he needed them to be special. I remembered how he would come home and go through all the cards, and eat only some of the candy. I remembered how much he loved his Valentine's gifts from me, or maybe, just the fact I always gave him one.

I remembered how much I loved him, and how much he loved me. I thought of how much I still love him, and how much he still loves me. In these moments of reflection, I painfully remembered how deeply I

94

miss him, and how very wrong the world feels without him in it.

This was my First Valentine's Day without Ryan ...

Blog Entry:

Tuesday, February 22, 2011

Five Months Later

As I begin to write, I reflect deeply upon the past 5 months. As each anniversary approaches, I remember every detail: the evening before Ryan died, the last words we shared together, and the unforgettable moments of September 22, 2010. Whether I want them to or not, these memories forcefully come flooding into my heart on the 22nd of each month. I also reflect on the journey thus far, examining each step my family and I have taken along the way. I remember each tear shed, each tear hidden, the fears which have surfaced, the anger which has risen, and the overwhelming sadness which has consumed each and every one of us at various times.

I remember when Ryan died, although I did not know what was ahead of me, or how I would manage to survive; I instinctively knew I would never be the same woman. When I look over the past 5 months, this is something which now resounds through me. I am NOT the same woman and never again will I be.

A specific area of change which seems to consume my thoughts the most at this time is the fact that I no longer feel real joy or happiness. I may smile or even laugh on a rare occasion. But despite these appearances, and/or surface feelings, my heart does not feel the joy it once did. It does not feel the happiness which permeates through one's heart and soul, making the world seem right. This in no way is a reflection on my other children; I love them all as intensely as I did before. In fact, I am sure they pay

*the price of the changes in me. For that, I am sorry.
I continue to give them all I have left, but I'm afraid it
may not be enough.*

*It used to be that whatever pain I experienced,
whatever challenges I faced, I did it with the
certainty I was strong, my heart was whole, and I
was blessed beyond measure. From this, I had the
knowledge that my life was complete, and I would be
happy again, no matter what the current challenge
may have been. I am not that same person. I may
be strong, but my heart is certainly not whole. What
use to be complete in my life is now torn apart. A
part of me died with my son, and I am left
fragmented. How could my life ever be complete
again with one of my children gone? How could my
heart ever feel whole again after losing one of my
babies? How could I ever experience real joy or
happiness, when there is an eternal sadness and
longing in my soul?*

*I sometimes think I miss the fulfillment of complete
happiness. But in all honesty, I don't even
remember what it genuinely feels like. My world has
changed so much, the woman I am has been so
altered, that I honestly don't remember how it felt to
be "me" before Ryan died. Sad thing is I don't even
have the desire to feel complete joy or happiness
anymore. I don't have the longing to do things
which once brought me pleasure. I won't pretend to
know how I will feel 6 months — or 6 years — from
now. But what I do know is this: at 5 months, this is
who I am. Right now, this IS me.*

Blog Entry:

Wednesday, March 16, 2011

A Birthday Letter to Ryan

My Dearest Ryan,

*As I write this letter to you, I reflect with deep love
on all the birthdays I was blessed to have you with
me. I remember your first birthday; I remember your*

*last. Your "last birthday" came far too soon. With
each year, although themes and presents would
change, one thing was constant: I was always so
happy to be celebrating your life. Your life, your
importance in mine and all who knew you, was
always a reason for celebration. Your 17th birthday
has arrived; only this time you are not here with me.*

*I always tried to think of ways to make you feel
special, gifts that I knew would make you happy. I
found such joy in these simple things because I
knew they would bring you happiness. To see you
smile always filled my heart with complete joy. This
year I am simply lost. For the first time, I don't know
what to do on March 17th. I don't know how to keep
from crying. I don't know how to celebrate "your
day" without you here, but I know I must. I don't
know how to make the day good for your brothers
and sisters, when I feel such a longing and sadness
within. I know I need to do something, because they
need to understand your life will always be worth
celebrating. I'm sure I will find my way, knowing you
are with me.*

*My sweet Ryan, I want you to know how much I love
you. How much I miss having you here each and
every day. How much I miss your footsteps walking
down the hallway every evening as you went to
wash your face. How much I miss your asking me,
"What's for dinner?" How much I miss the late night
sounds of the microwave, as you made yourself a
snack before bed. How much I miss your examining
of your hair after I gave you a haircut. How much I
miss our talks in your room. How much I miss
driving in the car with you and just visiting with each
other. How much I miss your openness with me.
How much I miss the way you would light up at
Christmas. How much I miss your excitement when
we went on vacations. How much I miss your eyes,
your hair, your smile and your hugs. How much I
miss hearing you tell me you love me. Just how
much I miss all of you, and the completeness you
brought into my life just by being you.*

I also want to tell you how much I respect and admire you. You were young when you left, but your soul was old. You taught so many how to live. You loved without conditions, you gave without expecting, you accepted without judgment. You held strong to your beliefs and convictions, and I admire that in you. You made me proud; you continue to make me proud.

So on your 17th birthday — March 17, 2011 — I celebrate and give thanks for your life. I celebrate the gifts you gave so freely to all you met. I celebrate the "one love" which was you. I celebrate your heart, your soul, your spirit. I thank God for you. Happy Birthday, my little boy. I love you. I love you completely and for all eternity. Being your mom is a sacred gift and a profound honor in my life. I deeply thank you for being my sweet and loving Ryan.

Mom

Blog Entry:

Tuesday, August 2, 2011

Another School Year Approaches

It seems like yesterday when Middletown High School called to ask if they could dedicate a yearbook page to Ryan. I was so touched and honored, not so much for myself but for Ryan. This kind and loving gesture spoke so clearly to me of the impact Ryan had on so many lives. Now, the first summer without him has come and gone, and a new school year is about to begin. The summer, which Ryan always loved, felt lonely. I found myself reflecting on last summer and all the joy Ryan experienced. I missed him here with me. As the school year approaches, my heart is filling with sadness of what could have been.

This school year would have been Ryan's senior year, a year he was so looking forward to. School shopping one last time, senior pictures, the joy of knowing it's your last year, celebrating with friends, choosing the path you want after school ends, the senior trip, the senior prom, and the moment of graduation, that moment of pride, success, accomplishment and freedom — experiences which we all assume our children will have, are now just painful reminders of what could have been.

All of the possibilities and opportunities that awaited him have been taken away. Although I know he is happy now and feel so much gratitude for his peace, I can't help but think about all of the life he will never live. He was at the threshold of new beginnings, and it all came to a sudden end. As I watch his friends begin to talk about and celebrate their senior year, and as we begin to prepare for the new school year, I am left with such a deep sadness. I know the year will be hard, and I will feel the struggle with every important step I watch his friends take. Although I will celebrate their joy, and sincerely wish them love and happiness, I will also feel the sadness of Ryan missing each of those steps. That reality is already piercing my heart. I will walk with, and encourage, his friends. I know Ryan would want me to do that. In doing so, perhaps I will help keep Ryan with them on their journeys.

I know God's Grace has carried me this far, and I pray it will continue to carry me. I pray I will be able to walk through what would have been Ryan's senior year with a sense of dignity, courage and strength. Even more than this, may I continue to honor Ryan, and the legacy he left, with every breath I take.

Blog Entry:

Friday, August 26, 2011

Eleven Months of Surviving

I find it very hard to believe 11 months have come and gone since the day my world was changed forever. I have carried pain which words are incapable of expressing. Words always came so easily to me, and now they don't seem to hold enough meaning to accurately express what my heart feels so deeply. The words seem to carry the same emptiness I feel within my very being. Despite this, my words and writing seem to be the only way to release some of the turmoil, which seems to build with each passing day. I think people probably assume it is getting easier, that I'm doing fine. They see me smile and carry on with life. If they don't ask, I don't share. I'm sure many of them have lost people in their lives and probably compare losing a child to that grief. I, too, have lost many people in my life, and it has hurt deeply. But losing a child does not compare to any other loss I have endured. Losing a child is in an unspeakable world of it's own. It literally turns your world upside down and inside out. If you haven't experienced it, you can't begin to understand the devastation. I completely understand and respect that reality. When they say it's the hardest loss there is, they are right. You don't get over it and move on. You just don't. Sadly, some people actually feel it works that way. They obviously have never lost a child or those thoughts would never cross their minds, or words pass through their lips. Since I will never get over it, I suppose all I can do is survive. Each day brings the painful challenge to do just that.

As the one-year anniversary approaches, I am filled with anxiety and sadness. I am feeling the devastation that is about to come, as if it hadn't happened yet. As the time approaches, I am triggered daily by things which take me back to the horror which no one should have to live through.

100

Each day brings tears, prompted by many different triggers. The sadness builds, and the tears increase. The day I lost Ryan, I wondered how I would ever survive. I knew I was changed as a woman forever, even though I did not know what that meant for me. Eleven months later, I still don't know what it means, yet I know I am very different. I AM surviving, but in all honesty (and contrary to what most people believe) the reality and devastation of this tragedy grows stronger with time. Perhaps the shock is slowly wearing off. The protections of those walls are beginning to fall, and it leaves me afraid, alone, empty, heartbroken and so incredibly sad.

Blog Entry:

Monday, September 12, 2011

As One Year Approaches

The days seem to be so very long right now, while the nights, which are my escape, become shorter. So many thoughts and feelings rush through me each day. I find myself lost in thoughts of Ryan, the day he was taken from my arms, how we have each survived the pain thus far, all the living Ryan will miss, and the painful realization that I have to live the rest of my life on this earth without him here with me. Sometimes that reality alone is almost too much to endure.

As the anniversary date approaches, I find my emotions are very raw, and my anxiety continues to build. I go through my day and do what is expected of me, but I can't seem to do more than that. My motivation and focus is almost nonexistent as I move through each passing day. At work, I find myself staring off, lost in thoughts. At times I feel utterly stunned by losing Ryan, and at other times the tears come without warning. At those moments I am consumed in anguish and do all I can to hide from the feelings. The pain, loss and sadness is just

101

too much at times. It feels as if I have no control over what I think or feel anymore. I am just swept away like a tide in an ever-changing ocean — turning, pushing, pulling, crashing, exploding on rocks, calmly retreating, only to repeat the turmoil once again. I am learning I can't fight it. Rather, I have to accept the emotional turmoil which is now my life.

I have no doubt the painful reality of losing Ryan is what begins to fill me now. I would give my life to change this reality, to bring my little boy home again. Sadly, this possibility is not mine. To hold him close, look into his beautiful blue eyes so full of life, glory in his contagious smile, hear his calming voice, drown in his beautiful laughter, tell him I love him, and hear him tell me the same — these are now just memories. What use to be part of my daily life are now just memories and dreams. I can't imagine anything more sad than that. I miss my sweet boy so very much.

Blog Entry:

Wednesday, September 21, 2011

One Year

I had no idea of what to expect as this time and date approached, although I had been warned of the turmoil that awaited me. I have learned over the past year NOT to be surprised at what each day may hold, or where my emotions may take me. This grief seems to have a life of its own, and I have tried very hard to just accept that hard fact.

Today, the eve of the One Year, I feel just as I did a year ago. The only difference is I don't have the shock to mysteriously protect me. I miss the shelter it provided, but know I must move forward with this heart-wrenching reality, no matter how painful it is. And it is more painful than words could ever express.

Physically, I have an endless pit in my stomach, my head is pounding relentlessly, and I feel nauseous. Emotionally, I feel the gut wrenching panic, the disbelief, the uncertainty, the isolation, the endless fear, the overwhelming concern for my other kids, the self-doubt in my ability to survive, the moments of not caring if I do, and the indescribable sadness in my heart and soul. My little boy is gone and my life on this earth will never be the same without him physically here. What does that mean for me? For us? I still don't have that answer; I only know we have all changed so very deep within.

Others may think I should be focusing on the good memories right now. I try very hard to do that, although it never takes away the sadness. Sometimes it brings moments of joy, and other times it actually makes it harder. Right now, in this moment, I am incapable of focusing on memories. What was once my life with Ryan is now only memories. The loss in that is so overwhelming at this stage, that all I can do is just breathe.

I have witnessed great pain in my other children. Pain I could not take away but only try to help them through. In recent days I have seen that pain surfacing with great force. I realize in those moments that they, like myself, just try to carry on, all the while the sadness is deep inside and never gone.

I have spent a lot of time today remembering the day before Ryan died: the talking we did, the dinner he ate, going into his room numerous times to check on him, him coming out to me with questions or things to share, the last words I said to him, and him to me. In 30 minutes, it will be a year since I last talked to Ryan, since I last heard his sweet and loving voice. The intensity of missing him is so fierce, I cannot even find words to describe it.

The one thing I am so very grateful for is I have not one regret. Ryan knew how much I loved him, and I knew how much he loved me. Our relationship was close, open and honest. We had a respect for each

*other which I will always carry. We often talked
about how we really understood each other. We
were so similar, in so many ways, that our hearts
instinctively knew each other on a level we didn't
even understand. I understand now, and I know he
does, too.*

*One Year. I have survived and grown spiritually; we
all have. But at this painful moment in the journey, I
feel as I did the day Ryan died. I feel broken.*

Blog Entry:

Monday, October 17, 2011

The "Firsts" Are Over?

*I have just passed the anniversary of Ryan's
Memorial (Oct 15th), so the "firsts" are officially
over. At least that is what I am told. I survived each
new month without him, my first birthday, the first
birthdays of my other children, the first holidays,
Ryan's first birthday, the first Mother's Day, and the
painful and devastating first anniversary of his
death. I knew each of these firsts would be a
slippery stepping stone which I would never forget,
but I also hoped somehow once the "firsts" were
completed, a glimmer of light would appear in my
world again, that somehow I would miraculously feel
whole again. I was very, very wrong.*

*Each morning when I wake, I hit my snooze button
and think of Ryan. I wonder how I will survive
another day, if I will manage again to forge through
the emptiness or if I will find a reason to smile. The
alarm goes off again, and I force myself up and
begin to go through the motions of yet another day.
Going through the motions — that seems to be all I
do now. I go to work, giving all I am capable of
giving, wondering if I'll ever feel the passion I use to
feel. I get home and do what needs to be done,
again giving all I am capable of giving: homework,
dinner, showers, attention, all the while looking*

104

forward to crawling into my bed, the place I can be alone and NOT pretend to be someone I no longer am. I'm still unsure of who I am or what I'm meant to be, but it is very clear I spend most of my day being what people think I should be or perhaps what I think they need me to be. Somehow I have gotten lost, and I'm not sure if anyone even realizes that.

This is a time of year I always loved. The season is changing, and with it seems to bring a comfort of being at home more with my family. With that comes the realization that the holidays are coming, another time to focus on my children, all their joy and love. Now this time of year haunts me. I have a painfully, piercing understanding that nothing is right inside my heart anymore, and I can't imagine how it ever could be again. My child is gone; nothing is right. With this realization comes a darkness I cannot even begin to describe. In fact, it is so overwhelming at times that I put great effort into pushing it away, hoping and praying one day I'll feel strong enough to face it. It literally takes my breath away.

What I have come to realize is this: each and every day is a "first" day without Ryan. There is no relief, no glimmer of light, no sense of wholeness, and no feelings of accomplishment for surviving the "firsts." For me, the "firsts" are never ending.

Chapter 6

Learning to Move Forward

Blog Entry:

Friday, November 25, 2011

The Second Thanksgiving

For many different reasons, we decided to stay home for Thanksgiving, surrounding ourselves in the peace of our own home. Sean and Kaitie were at their dad's house, so it was just the four of us. I spent the day cooking, trying to stay focused on that alone. It was very nice, and I thought I had gotten through it quite well overall. The older kids came over in the evening, which was very comforting. When I went to bed, I realized how much I had controlled my emotions and thoughts that day, how I deliberately tried to focus on what was at hand versus what I was missing. I had succeeded; but when I lay in the quiet, I could not escape the sadness of what was missing, my Ryan. I felt so deeply sad as I lay there in the realization that holidays would never be as they once were. How do I deal with that?

Today I started pulling out the Christmas decorations. I knew if I didn't get that ball rolling quickly, I wouldn't want to do it at all. Last year as I began that process, I was doing it to make things as normal as I could for the other kids. Today as I did it, I felt it was more of a habit then anything. I moved slowly, felt very anxious inside, and just wanted to do what I had to do — and do it alone. I remembered how I would always play Christmas music and make a fun day of decorating. It felt so joyful to fix the house up. It brought comfort, peace and love to all of us. Today I just went through the motions, AGAIN, going through the motions. I heard the neighbors doing lights outside, all together in laughter and completeness. I remember those days and that complete joy. Although I can remember the joy, I can't remember what it felt like. That is the sad reality of what has happened to my heart. I have spent most of the day crying, as I pushed myself through, doing what I needed to do, making things as normal as I could for everyone else.

We often took family pictures at this time of year and used it for our Christmas card. We haven't taken a family picture since Ryan died, and quite honestly I don't know when I will ever be able to do that again, if ever. How do you take a family picture when one of your children is now gone?

I spent most of the first year making sure my kids and husband were all right, at least as all right as they could be. I continue to do this, but I also spend more time looking within. I must say, it's a very sad place to look. I realize I am still taking One Small Step at a Time. I don't know that I have made any progress with this grief. I don't know if that's even possible. I have gone through all "the firsts," and here it is the second Thanksgiving. It honestly feels worse than it did last year. I genuinely believe that has something to do with the shock factor and the protection it provides. Maybe part of it is also the fact that since it's been a year, many people naturally assume you are better. Maybe it's both? I really don't know, and to be honest, I guess it really doesn't matter; it just is. Life feels very lonely right now.

I look at this picture, and I realize things will never be whole for me again. One of my babies is gone, and a large part of me went with him. So events which focus on family — Thanksgiving, Christmas, Easter, birthdays, family gatherings — all just magnify the fact that life is NOT the same. It will never be again. Ryan is gone. My son has died, and that has forever changed me and my life. Today I am really feeling the devastating pain of that reality.

Blog Entry:

Saturday, December 31, 2011

Another New Year

It's New Year's Eve again, another one without Ryan here. I look back over the past year and realize that although I remember so many details, I also remember nothing. It is a year of my life which came and went, with little heartfelt participation by me. I did my best under the circumstances, so I make no apologies.

I have learned a lot over the past year. I have learned what REAL friends are, and I am FOREVER grateful for those people in my life. I have heard people say they didn't know what to say, which I so genuinely appreciated. I have also heard the deafening silence of others. I have watched people endlessly try to show their support through words or actions. I have witnessed those who chose not to do either. I have been blessed by people who freely and lovingly talk about, and listen to me, as I talk about my son. I have been deeply hurt by those who don't speak of him, or seem to listen as I do. I have been greatly blessed by Ryan's friends; their love for

108

Ryan has carried me through the darkest of days, and continue to do so. They love, honor and remember him always. I could never thank them enough for showing me how important he was, and still is, in their lives. In return, they have become very important in mine. I have learned again how incredible my family is. They have been there, and continue to be there, as this painful journey continues. They can't heal me, as much as they wish they could; but they have shown me over and over that Ryan really mattered to them, and that my hurting heart also matters. What a gift they have given me. Ryan would be proud.

Probably the greatest thing I have learned is to take care of myself, to love myself. Being in such a broken place, you realize how important it is to take care of yourself because you are so vulnerable and fragile. I have learned to do things to nurture my spirit, and I do them — trips to the coast, writing my blog, time alone, allowing the tears to come, listening to my heart, etc. I have learned who to let close and who to keep distant, all out of doing what is best for my heart and soul. I have learned to set boundaries, protecting my heart and the heart of my family. I never tolerated judgmental people very well, but now I have no tolerance, so I keep those people clear of my life. I am learning that it does not matter what people think of me — something Ryan had already understood. As Ryan once said to me, "I know my heart, and if someone is judging me and chooses not to see it, that's their loss." In all of this, I am learning to love myself the way I know I am supposed to.

So as another new year approaches, I am feeling very solemn and nostalgic. I am missing Ryan more with each day. What I thought would get easier is, in fact, getting harder. In this sadness, I am also trying to see the gifts I have been given. I know Ryan would want me to nurture and love myself. I KNOW that. I will continue to try to do this. I want to make him proud.

Sunday, January 29, 2012

Strength In Tragedy

During the past year I have questioned my strength and endurance numerous times. What I considered to be strong before doesn't seem to be strength now. What I use to see as weakness now glimmers with the light of strength. When you are faced with the tragedy of losing a child, you are given a lifetime of challenges to overcome, or at least endure. In these challenges, you continually question yourself in every step you take. Am I doing this right? Can I really survive? Will I ever really feel joy again? Am I helping my kids to endure what they should never have had to endure? Do I have the strength?

Is it being strong to put your mask on and move forward as if things are normal, or is real strength removing that mask and letting everyone know you no longer have a normal existence? Is it being strong to stand upright with a smile on your face, or is real strength letting the tears flow and anxiety show? Is it strong to celebrate the joy of your son's friends, or is real strength admitting that although you are happy for them, it breaks your heart that your son is missing out on all of the celebrations? Is it strong to act like it doesn't hurt deeply when people don't speak about your son anymore, or is real strength speaking up and saying you need them to talk about him or at least acknowledge it when you do? Is it strong to pretend you're not hurt by those who don't reach out, or is real strength admitting you are, and then setting boundaries for yourself so you can't be hurt anymore than you already have been? Is it strong to forge forward on those days you can barely get out of bed, or is real strength staying in bed and allowing yourself to just feel the sadness you are so deeply afraid of? Is it strong to say your son is in a better place, at peace and completely happy, or is real strength knowing this, yet still being able to say the pain of missing

110

him is overwhelming, devastating and all consuming? Is it strong to bravely face all your daily responsibilities, or is real strength taking time out to nurture your bleeding soul? What is strength in tragedy?

I don't know the answers, but I do know I have done all of the above. With the Grace of God, I am still here and manage to make it through each day. I continue to take life "one small step at a time" and praying I will find the strength to face each day with some sense of dignity and grace.

Blog Entry:

Friday, April 26, 2013

Some Lessons Learned

Over the past two and a half years, I've learned so many things. Some are painful, some bring hope.

I have learned that I am stronger than I realized. I have survived the greatest loss you could ever experience as a parent. At times I still don't know how I will face the next day. There are days I find it hard to breathe, but somehow I do. With the love of those close to me, and through God's grace, I have somehow helped to walk my kids through the deepest darkness of their lives. As a mother to them all, I feel so grateful for that.

I have learned how loving my children are. They have lost their brother, yet have poured their hearts into Ryan's Memorial Fund, finding such peace in giving to others, all in their brother's name and honor. They have walked through such darkness; and although they will always feel that loss, they also have learned that they can feel joy again. They continue to love others, even though love was ripped out of their lives.

111

I have learned that some people will walk by your side and support you for the rest of your life. They will tell you how much Ryan meant to them, or speak his name with love. They show their love for me, my family, and for Ryan, with their actions and words. In doing this, they show that his life here DID matter, and in no way is he forgotten. THOSE are the people that carry me, my husband and my kids through each day. I have also learned there are those who do not speak his name or even acknowledge it when spoken by us. That is hurtful. I am still learning how to let that go. We all are.

I have learned, after losing my child, I can endure ANY pain or loss.

I have learned that Ryan's beliefs and attitudes were beyond his age. His belief in "One Love" is the way we should all live. I continue to learn from his life.

I have learned through my other kids that there can still be joy in life. It may be different; it may be for mere moments at a time, but it is there.

I am still learning to live my new "normal" life — whatever that means. There is a huge hole in my heart, and in our family as a whole, but we are learning to live with that. We are doing the best we can do.

I am still learning to understand the woman I have become since losing Ryan. I have learned that I may spend the rest of my life here trying to understand who I have become, or am still becoming, but I have also learned that is all right.

I have learned how important it is to take time to nurture myself. When your heart and spirit have been broken like this, you need to find a place where you can breathe and feel the calmness that peace brings. When you find that place, you need to take yourself there often. I am learning to do just that.

I have learned that this journey I am on truly is just "One small step at a time."

Blog Entry:

Friday, September 27, 2013

Living the Could Have Beens

It's hard to believe that Kaitie is now the same age Ryan was when he died. Time continues on, and with it comes new challenges we must all face.

We just passed the anniversary of Ryan's death. This year held a lot of added anxiety due to Kaitie's age. It was hard for her, hard for me. We talked about the turmoil this was causing, and we had faced the fears which it brought together. I have always had close relationships with my kids, and this was one of those times I felt very grateful for that gift.

I have thought many times about the things Ryan would never do in his life. As I watched his classmates take their senior pictures, go on their senior trips, and graduate, sadness filled me. I thought it was past me after graduation, and then Kaitie turned 16. I realize now I will be living a lifetime of "could have beens" as I watch her grow.

I have thought deeply about how to handle this. I don't want to take away from Kaitie's joys and milestones, yet I can't hide what each step stirs deep in my soul. I have accepted the fact that I will feel both joy and sadness as she journeys through her life. I have decided to make each milestone extra special for Kaitie, as if she were living it for two. Doing this has not taken away the sadness, but it has helped lighten the load. I pray it continues to ease some of the sadness as I move forward celebrating Kaitie's life, yet "living the could have beens."

Blog Entry:

Sunday, May 21, 2012

The Pain of My Children

The time has moved forward, whether we wanted it to or not. Everyone wears a smile, a mask. Is it to put on a front for others, or is it to put on a front for ourselves?

I have been fairly open with my own journey through this darkness. Although, in all honesty, I haven't even allowed myself to go to that lonely, painful place for more than seconds at a time. It is too hard, too sad, too dark, too empty, too much. I have tried to help my kids as much as I can. But even with me, they wear their masks. I suppose I wear it with them as well. Perhaps we're all too afraid to show each other how we really feel, afraid we will bring each other into that place where none of us are ready to go. Little by little they share their tears. I share mine. In watching my kids move forward so bravely, yet suffer so silently, I am learning that we have to go to that place we are so afraid of, even if it's a little bit at a time. We have no choice; the masks are beginning to tear as the reality of what is takes over.

Loss of focus, loss of dreams, loss of passions, loss of closeness with people. Anger, sadness, physical illnesses, constant fear with every breath taken. This is what has become of my children. These are my children, and I love them. I sadly know the greatest pain a mother could endure is the loss of her child. I believe the second is to watch her children suffer. I know my own mom has carried that pain as she witnessed my heart break, and I am witnessing that very pain in my own children. At times it feels overwhelming, yet somehow I find the strength to be there for and with them. I ask God to help me, and I keep trying.

They have all had their worlds turned upside down. They have had their very hearts broken apart, their dreams of the future ripped into a million pieces. They have tried to move on and have done so as well as could be expected. They have shown great courage, strength and grace. But they are wounded, traumatized and forever changed. Like me, they are NOT the same people they were before they lost their brother. Over the past few months, as their masks have worn thin, I have seen glimpses of the deep pain they carry still: confusion of not knowing how to get through the next day, sometimes not even caring if they do; the painful reality that their brother is really gone; the longing for what could have been and should have been; the anger of it all, which no doubt is in reality the unspeakable sadness they carry; the constant fear of dying or of losing me, which manifests itself relentlessly; and the need to talk about the pain, yet fear of going into that darkness.

115

My children are in pain. Anyone close enough to them sees what they try so hard not to show. Those are the friends I am so grateful they have. I will continue to do all I can to help them, but I know I can't make it better. That is hard, but it is the truth. They are all so very close, and one of them is missing. They all feel the loss with great intensity and sadness. I just pray God holds them all, while He leads me. The Pain of My Children...it's unimaginable.

Blog Entry:

Wednesday, January 2, 2013

Ryan's Senior Year

The 2011-2012 school year is a year I will never forget. What would have been Ryan's senior year, a time of joy and celebration, in fact was a time of great sorrow. As much happiness as I felt for all of his friends, I felt an even heavier sadness. I was bluntly faced with all that Ryan was missing. With every senior picture, excitement about the senior trip, pictures of seniors dressed up for prom, dreams of their futures, and preparing for their high school graduation, my heart would drop so deep inside that I felt I would never be able to reach it again.

My Ryan did not get to take senior pictures, he did not get to go to his senior prom, he didn't experience the great adventures of a senior trip, and his dreams of college and life after high school were taken away. He was weeks away from getting his driver's license -- all requirements done, just waiting out the time. He would never graduate from high school. His life was suddenly cut short, and we were left with the pain of all the things he never did, nor would ever have the chance to do.

A couple of weeks before graduation, the principal at Middletown High School, Mr. Roderick, called me in. He informed me that he had ordered a diploma for Ryan. I immediately began to cry; somehow my baby would graduate! I was overwhelmed with the compassion this man had, not only for our family but for all the graduating seniors. We all needed closure with this graduation. Mr. Roderick knew this and did what he could to help all involved. He informed me they would have a chair, which would be empty, in Ryan's honor. He asked if Kaitie would accept the diploma for Ryan. Again, I cried. Kaitie sat in the chair for Ryan as the class walked in; none of the graduates knew she would be there. Then the diploma, which his classmates knew nothing about, was presented to Kaitie. There were cheers, whistles, and so many tears. She accepted it with such strength, courage and grace. I was so very proud of her, and I knew Ryan was too. After she accepted the diploma, she sat down with me, leaving Ryan's chair empty. It was then that she began to cry. As I looked through my tears to Kaitie, and to Ryan's classmates, I saw the gift of closure Mr. Roderick gave to them all. Our Ryan was graduating with his class.

This journey has been so very painful, and I'm afraid it is not getting easier. One thing I have learned as I face each day is that there are people along the way who reach out and somehow know exactly what to say or do -- whether it's to let you know they don't know what to say but are there for you, or to share a story or memory of Ryan, or to acknowledge him on his birthday, holidays or any gathering of family or friends, or to respectfully honor our son at graduation. Each word or action is to let you know they have NOT forgotten your child, that he mattered in this life ... and he still does. I can't thank those people enough. I will never forget what Mr. Roderick did for all of us at the graduation of 2012. He honored my son, and in doing that, he let me know that Ryan did matter and is NOT forgotten. At the end of each day, that is all that really helps, all I really want, all I really need.

Blog Entry:

Thursday, January 3, 2013

Our First Family Vacation

I knew the time would come when we would take a family vacation without Ryan, but I didn't know how intense the pain would be until I got there.

Sadly for us all, my selflessly loving mom died in June. My sister asked me to come to Disneyland with them at Thanksgiving, as it would be her first time back there without my mom. I wanted to help her, and I also knew my kids needed some joy in their lives. We thought we would be helping each other to take a hard step for both of us, and we knew my mom and Ryan would be so happy about that. However, I knew in my heart I wasn't ready for this. Disneyland was the last place we took a family vacation WITH Ryan. How could I go back to the place he loved so much WITHOUT him? Despite my overwhelming fears, I knew we had to go.

The kids were all very happy, so I felt I was doing the right thing for them. I learned quickly that sometimes what is good for your kids may not be good for you. Being a mom, you put your kids first in most situations. Since Ryan died, I have tried so hard to do whatever was right for them, whatever I could do to help heal their broken hearts. They had to come first. I needed to help them move forward even though I didn't know how to do it myself.

When we entered Disneyland, someone took a family picture of us. When I looked at it, the first family picture without Ryan, I began to cry. We have not taken family pictures since Ryan died, and it is very clear to me why. That was the beginning of the end for me. I literally cried my way through the happiest place on earth for three days! I didn't know when it would happen or what would set me off. I just knew when it hit I needed to walk off by myself. I know the younger kids were in their own world and enjoying every second. But the older kids saw the pain in me; they understood it, and they carried it as well.

When I look at the picture of Sean and Kaitie at Disneyland, I see my two beautiful children, but I also see the one who is missing. Does anyone else see what this mother's heart sees? Instead of Ryan's "light up the world" smile next to his brother and sister's smiles, his ashes are in the tattoo in Sean's arm. What has happened to my once perfect and complete family?

I feel somehow I let everyone down this vacation. My sister, who asked me to be there — I was emotionally unavailable to her. Sean and Kaitie, who needed joy more than anyone, witnessed their mother's heart break all over again. My husband, who wants nothing more than to wash away all my pain, saw how deep it actually was, how successfully I hide it, and how helpless it leaves him.

I learned that I do keep so much of this sadness buried within. It's the only way for a mother's heart to survive such a loss, I believe. You literally take it one small step at a time. You let yourself feel as much as you can handle feeling at any given moment, and then you close down. If you don't close down when you feel the need, it will consume you, and the fear of where that will take you is too much to even think about. I learned that listening to my heart about what I can and can't handle is what I *have to continue to do. It's one way that I can take care of myself, and I know Ryan wants that.*

The little ones had a great time. My older kids said they had fun, too, despite my breakdowns. I hope this is true. If I brought them any joy at all by taking them on vacation to Disneyland, then I know I did the right thing ... even if it wasn't right for me.

Blog Entry:

Saturday, September 21, 2013

Three Years Missing You

Tomorrow will be three years since I lost my son ... three years of missing him. I remember and relive this evening as each year passes -- the last moments I spent with Ryan on this earth. They are so vivid, so clear, yet so long ago.

As September 1 hits, the anxiety begins to build within. A silence fills my heart. With each passing day, the sadness and anxiety grow within. I wonder if I will survive each day, but then remember I feel this way every September, and I do survive.

This anniversary date is holding much turmoil, not only for me, but for Kaitie. My little girl is now the same age and grade in school that Ryan was when he died. With that reality comes much fear, worry, sadness and heartache. Kaitie is carrying an anxiety and fear no one could understand. My heart aches for the journey she is on right now and has been on for so long now. She is strong and courageous but, like myself, carries her pain within. As a mom, I look at her, and I remember Ryan. She is exactly where he was when he died. I can't even express how that feels and weighs in my heart.

I feel as though I have endured this year better than last year. I'm not sure if I'm just learning to survive with more grace or if I'm just burying my broken heart with more ease. With tears rolling down my face as I type this, I think I probably just bury the heartache with more ease. Pushing the pain down is one of the ways to survive each day. It really is too much to endure; I can only handle little bits at a time.

How do you ever accept, or get over, the fact that your child died? You don't. How do you ever find peace within your soul, when such a large part of it is gone? You don't. How do you feel safe when you go to bed each night knowing that one of your children died in his sleep? You don't. How do you ever feel peace within your heart, when your heart has been shattered? You don't. You just learn to live with it. You learn to endure the heartache. You learn to live your life as it is now and carry the emptiness within. You try to be the best you can be with what you have left, knowing inside it is not at all the person you were before. You move forward because you have to, not necessarily because you want to.

Losing a child is a lifetime grieving process. It's something you live through each and every day. It's been three years. Yes, I am surviving. Yes, I am living life. Yes, I am trying the best I can. Yes, I have learned to laugh again. However, the longing, the sadness, the missing, the emptiness, the heartache are all very much alive within. That is who I am now, whether people see it or not. This is my life now.

As I type these last words, I realize it is exactly 3 years (10:30 pm) since I last spoke to, and saw, my Ryan alive on this earth. I miss him more than I can express.

Friday, January 3, 2013

The Third Christmas without Ryan

With a feeling of relief, I write that our third Christmas without Ryan has come and gone. I can't say it's easier, but I can say I am learning how to get through it with more grace. I am learning how to survive a holiday that he loved so much. I'm learning to do it while carrying the endless ache for him in my heart.

Over the past three years, I have learned what I need to do to somehow make Christmas tolerable for us all. My kids have always come first, so making sure things were as close to normal is what I have tried to do. The sad thing is, our normal is not the same, so we have all struggled in trying to find a new way.

Christmas is especially hard because it is a time of family, love, joy and togetherness. When a child is missing from that family unit, nothing is right. How do we keep their spirits alive during this season so we can survive it? How do we cope with an empty stocking or a tree that once held all of his special ornaments? How do we decorate our house as we always have? All of these things bring great pain and deep turmoil.

I knew things had to stay the same, yet also change, so we could all get through it.

The first year we decided to write notes to put in Ryan's stocking. My husband came up with that idea when I fell apart at the idea of not filling his stocking for the first time. By doing this, his stocking would not be empty, but rather have something very special in it. This gave us each the opportunity to give Ryan a Christmas gift, as well as have sacred time alone with him. It seemed to help us all; since then, each one of us looks forward to spending that special time with Ryan. And I KNOW Ryan loves that time with us. I keep the notes in his stocking all year; we add our new ones each Christmas. I also place his stocking in the center, surrounding it by the stockings of those who love and miss him most. It's another way to honor him -- a way to ease my heart.

Last year we decided to redesign our Christmas tree. We all had our special ornaments that I have been getting the kids since they were little. None of us felt good abou t putting them on the tree. It caused a lot of sadness. It was something we needed to change. We all decided we would make our tree purple -- Ryan's favorite color -- to honor him. I completely transformed the tree, and it has eased many hearts. It's Ryan's Tree, the center of our home at Christmas.

We used to leave the decorations up through the New Year, but I can't cope with that anymore. Once I manage to make it through Christmas, I have to remove the holiday as quickly as I can. I can't prolong a time that used to be complete joy, because it no longer is.

I am relieved to have survived another Christmas. It's sad to think it's about surviving it; but in all honesty, that's what most everything is about now. I have done what I need to do to make it less painful for everyone, including myself. These changes help us all to get through a time when Ryan's death is very heavy in our hearts -- a time he is so deeply missed. The third Christmas without Ryan has passed, and I am relieved.

Chapter 7

My Spiritual Search and Transformation

Blog Entry:

Friday, November 5, 2010

Hearts From Ryan

I have been feeling like Ryan is not near me for some reason. It's a very sad and lonely feeling. I have not seen hearts in the skies, or had whispers from God, over the past week. It has left me feeling very isolated. I have been sadly wondering: where has my Ryan gone?

Today I decided to go through my top drawer, to see if there was something in there from Ryan. I found a basketball pin, which I immediately placed on the dresser next to Ryan. I found three different cards he had given me or made me. Each card expressed his love, and on each card he drew a single heart or numerous hearts. From when he was very small, he would always draw a heart on his cards for me. I always thought it was sweet, but now I realize it was to be his sign to me, his sign to all. "One Love ... One Heart."

I then noticed two necklaces hanging above my dresser where Ryan rests. One was a necklace from Disneyland from about 7 years ago. I had given Ryan money to buy himself something; and when he came out of the store, he had spent the money on a gift for me -- a typical, giving gesture by Ryan. It was too small to wear, so I hung it up where it would be safe. Next to it was a necklace I had forgotten about, another gift from Ryan. I don't remember if it was Mother's Day or my birthday, but I suppose it doesn't matter. Ryan was upset he couldn't get me a gift and his brother Sean, who was working, could. He wanted to be able to show me he loved me the same way Sean did. So Russ took him shopping for me. He bought a heart-shaped necklace with "Mom" written inside the heart. He told me it said Mom for me, and the heart was because his heart belonged to me. His gesture took my breath away, and I remember feeling so loved at that moment. Today, when I found it, I felt even more loved. Again, it was a heart from Ryan.

Hanging in my hallway are a couple of pictures Ryan made in elementary school. I loved them so much I framed them. One is a very modern looking picture with geometrical shapes and a vase holding flowers in the middle. On the center of the vase is a single heart. I had never even noticed that heart being there before. I saw it today; I felt Ryan.

To top things off, looking into the sky this afternoon I saw three different hearts, all bunched in a group near each other. I knew Ryan was letting me know he IS here. He gave me an abundance of hearts today; and though they may seem meaningless to someone else, they mean the world to me. I think Ryan knows that.

Ryan's Message In a Dream

Ryan's friend sent me a note a couple of weeks ago. She had another dream that included Ryan. She said they were sitting together, and in the background a song was playing -- "Dear Mama." As the music played, the words appeared in front of her, much like they would on a karaoke machine. As the words scrolled down, Ryan grabbed the lyrics he liked, or he wanted her to share with me. When he touched the lyrics, they became brighter, came toward her, and then disappeared. When she woke, she felt she was meant to share the lyrics with me. I am grateful for this.

Some may think this is nothing but a nice dream; but for myself, I believe Ryan had something to share with me and, once again, he knew where to go. He knows my pain, could never bear to see me cry, and I believe he is reaching out once more, reaching out just to let me know how much he loved me and loves me still. Ryan had a message, and shared it through his friend's dream. This I BELIEVE.

> *"I finally understand, for a woman it ain't easy trying to raise a man.*
>
> *"Lady, don't you know we love you sweet lady? Place no one above you sweet lady. You are appreciated, don't you know we love you?*
>
> *"Cause when I was low you were there for me, and never left me alone cause you cared for me.*
>
> *"And I could see you coming home from work late, in the kitchen trying a fix us a hot plate.*

127

"Just working with the scraps you were given, mama made miracles every Thanksgiving.

" Pour out some liquor and I reminisce, cause through the drama I can always depend on my mama.

"And when it seems like I'm hopeless, you say the words that could get me back in focus.

"When I was sick as a little kid, to keep me happy there's no limit to the things you did.

"And all my childhood memories are full of all the sweet things you did for me.

"And even though I act crazy, gotta thank the lord that you made me.

"There are no words to explain the way I feel, you never kept secrets, always stayed real.

"And I appreciate how you raised me, and all the extra love that you gave me.

"I wish that I could take the pain away, if you can make it through the night, there's a better day.

"Everything will be all right if you hold on; it's a struggle every day, gotta roll on.

"And there's no way I can pay you back, but my plan is to show you that I understand. You are appreciated."

Blog Entry:

Saturday, January 8, 2011

A Message In a Dream

December 29th is the anniversary of my dad's death. On this day I found myself constantly thinking about my dad, as I always do; but this year, I also found myself with constant thoughts of Ryan. I wondered what they were doing. Were they spending time together? What do they do in Heaven? Do they miss us? Does Ryan miss me? Wondering if you are in the glory of Heaven, would you ever have the feelings of missing someone? -- just random thoughts and questions I have frequently, as I try to stumble through my life without him here.

I received an email from Ryan's friend, the one who has the meaningful dreams with Ryan in them. She told me she had another dream on the 29th (Coincidence? I don't think so). She said Ryan appeared to her again, specifically asking her to tell me something for him. When he was done telling her, he told her he loved her, and thanked her for sharing the other dreams with me. This is what he said:

> *"Goodbyes are not forever;*
>
> *Goodbyes are not the end.*
>
> *They just mean I'll miss you,*
>
> *Until we meet again.*
>
> *I love you mom, and miss you more than you know."*

Once again, I was left in awe. I did not share the thoughts, feelings and questions I was having this day with anyone. But somehow Ryan knew; and even more than this, he knew how important it was for me to know the answer. He continues to reach out, nurture and love. He is teaching me that even

129

though someone is in Heaven and living a life far more beautiful than we could ever imagine, they are still with us. They hear us; they know our thoughts and they feel our hearts. They continue to love us because even though the body is gone, the spirit lives on. The spirit is where love is born and lives; it never dies. This knowledge does not take away the sadness or pain of having him physically gone. It does not heal the brokenness I feel within. However, it does bring a sense of comfort and hope. It confirms my beliefs, and it opens my eyes so much wider.

A message in a dream -- I asked God to always help me hear what Ryan is saying or showing me, promising them both I will always have my heart and eyes open. Ryan is reaching out, and God is helping me to see and hear. I will keep my promise.

Blog Entry:

Monday,Birthday May 2, 2011

As Time Passes

As I look at pictures, I remember my baby, my son, so full of kindness, laughter and love. A smile that always managed to melt my heart and completely fill me with joy. I miss him more than I could ever express through tears, words or written language. Only a mother who has lost a child could ever know and understand my heart now. I have come to accept that fact, and it often leaves me in silence. I wonder why I should even try to explain how I feel; no one will understand anyway. Writing helps my heart to process what my mind still has a hard time accepting, yet that has become a challenge as well.

So many times I want to sit down, writing all the thoughts and feelings which swirl through my mind and heart each day. But I find my mind is fragmented, making writing a challenge. I can't seem to capture the words to express all that is

130

happening within, and to, me. I suppose this fragmentation is a painful reflection of my heart.

When Ryan's birthday came, I felt the walls thicken, growing even stronger. I shut myself in, walking through the day in darkness and fear -- fear that the pain would somehow find a way to escape. If I started crying, I may not stop this time, and I found that paralyzing. The wishes, prayers and love of those who dared to acknowledge his birthday to me, are literally what carried me through the day. For that, I am grateful. The 6-month anniversary, Easter, and the 7-month anniversary have all come since then.

Sadly, I still feel the lingering paralysis from that first birthday without him. He would have been 17.

Each day I force myself up and face the day, whether I am ready or not. Every evening, I process the emotions of the day, which often leaves me in complete exhaustion. The world has changed for me, for my family, and we all struggle to understand and accept our new reality. Words could never adequately express what our hearts have been required to endure.

My spiritual growth has taken me places many people would not believe. But because of my deep faith, and my love for Ryan, I have been gifted with a new understanding. Seeing what I have seen, my faith has grown even deeper than I ever dreamed possible. As a result, God has been taken right out of the box, the box so many of us put Him in, although we don't realize we've done it. For those gifts, I am eternally grateful. I have been shown, and given, gifts which will carry me through the rest of my life, only to better prepare me for what awaits when I go Home -- a place I look forward to returning to. This has been the gift I have been blessed with throughout this unspeakable sorrow.

Despite this precious gift, I am a human. I am a woman who has lost her child, at too young an age. I am a mother who takes care of my other kids, all of my daily responsibilities, goes to work each day, yet cries when I am alone and no one can see. I am only just learning to share my pain with those close to my heart, in little bits and pieces, as that's all I can bare at any given moment. I have strength beyond measure, but am still completely overwhelmed by the grief of losing Ryan. I am human. I am a grieving mother; and although I know it's not possible, sometimes I cry out to God to please give me back my little boy. It is in these moments I am painfully aware; this journey has only just begun.

Blog Entry:

Friday, November 19, 2010

What I Believe

I have spent a lot of time pondering my beliefs, the very beliefs that breathe life into me each day. During a time like this, you need your beliefs to fall on, to lean on, to hold you up. Beliefs are with you no matter what challenges life gives you, no matter how much anguish you feel, no matter how much you feel God is testing you. If you believe, your faith will carry you through. At least, that has been the reality in my life.

I believe in God. For as long as I can remember, that faith has been within me. Through joys, pains, sorrows and celebrations, it has been constant. My relationship with God has taken many roads throughout the years. It has been turbulent, quiet, fulfilling, full of question and life sustaining. No matter how much pain or loss I have felt, I have never questioned whether or not God existed. I just knew He did. When I lost Ryan, I remember thinking,"If ever I would question my beliefs, now will be the time." Despite my heart being broken, leaving me lifeless, I still believe. I don't understand why, but I don't need to understand -- that is what faith is about.

132

I also believe that with God all things are possible. I believe when someone you love dies, they watch over you. I believe they are always with you, and if you listen with an open heart and open mind, you will hear, see and feel the signs of love they send you. It may be through clouds, through a scent, through dreams, through music, through a feeling, through visions; we just need to listen. Some may think this is merely a grieving mother needing to see what she sees, reading things into nothing, but I say it is not. I KNOW it is not. After all, all things are possible with God. Are they not? Who are we on earth to put limits on what God can or will do to bring comfort to a crying heart?

My dad coming to me in a dream prior to Ryan's death just confirms my belief. I didn't know what the dream meant until after Ryan died, but now it is one of the only things that gives me comfort in knowing there was nothing I could have done. God's plan was already in motion. He sent me a message of "soon to be comfort" before Ryan died. He let my dad come to me, knowing I would turn back to that dream numerous times, just to get through each day. I believe my dad came to help me in the only way he could. He is in Heaven. I am on earth, but I am still his daughter. He knew the pain I was about to encounter and he needed to be there for his little girl. He was there for me -- for Ryan. That dream was a gift, a gift that has kept me breathing.

Prior to my surgery last week, I asked Ryan to be with me. The night of my surgery, one of Ryan's friends had a dream, which she shared with me. I found her note days later, and wrote back to her in tears. I shared that I had asked Ryan to be with me, that I had surgery, and assured her I would thank Ryan for sending me a message through her -- because I knew he had. I did thank him, and I know he heard, because this same girl had another dream just the other night. Ryan came to her and thanked her for letting me know how he felt. This was her note to me:

"I woke up crying from this dream and knew that I had to tell you. We were somewhere, I still can't figure out where, but there was beautiful green grass and a little waterfall that ran into a pond. It was sunny, but there was some wind, so it wasn't very hot. He was saying how much he cared for you and he said that you would be OK and he is with you. I couldn't figure out why he was saying you would be OK, but now I know it was because of your surgery. He started to cry when he started to say he doesn't think you know how much you meant to him and how much he loves you and how he loved your relationship. He said he knows you can get through anything because you are the strongest woman he has ever met. He also said that you were not only his mom, but his best friend, and he would give anything to have one more day with you so you know how much you mean to him."

When I read the note, I immediately broke into uncontrollable tears. I KNEW Ryan had come to her. He needed me to know something and he knew who to go to, someone who would hear, believe and share. Ryan knows my strong belief and faith in God, and all the possibilities that holds. Ryan shared that faith. I don't put limits on what is possible — I never have. I honestly do believe all things are possible with God. I have seen it in my life numerous times, and I am seeing it now, a time when I need it the most.

What do I believe? I believe in God, I believe our loved ones are always with us, and I believe if we have the open heart that is needed, they will reach out and we will hear, see and feel it. I do believe all things are possible. I believe because I have faith.

Thursday, October 28, 2010

Ryan's Journal Entry

About a week or two after Ryan died, I decided to open his backpack and empty it out. This is the only thing I have done so far — one step at a time I keep saying. In the front of his school binder was loose papers, which were journal entries, I'm assuming for his English class. I read through them all, so grateful to have little pieces of Ryan's heart and mind, treasures to keep, knowing they were his recent thoughts and feelings on various topics. One of the journals sent chills through me, It was written just days before he died.

> *"I've been thinking about what I want to do before I die for a long time. I've come to a conclusion that there are three specific things that I feel like I need to do before I die. The first thing I want to do is go skydiving. I'm into big thrills and I don't know of anything more accelerating than jumping out of an airplane. The only thing is that you have to be 18 to be able to do it, so I'm hoping I make it past 18. The second thing I want to do before I die is to travel the world. I've never been out of the U.S. and I'm interested in what other countries are like. The third thing that I want to do before I die is to get a meaningful tattoo. Probably something to do with my mom."*

Interesting enough, immediately after Ryan died, his dad and two older brothers, Jeremy and Sean, got tattoos in honor of Ryan — "a meaningful tattoo." Since Ryan mentioned his tattoo probably would have something to do with me, I am also thinking of some small tattoo I could get to honor my little boy, giving to him what I know he wanted to give to me. Ryan's sister and brother (Shawndre' and Sean) plan to live out Ryan's dream and go skydiving one day soon. I will go with them so I can share in their bittersweet moments of living out their little brother's dream for him and so I can tell them how incredibly proud I am that they would do that for Ryan. Ryan's little sister, Kaitie, asked how she could live out a dream. I told her that Ryan wanted to travel so perhaps she could be the one that traveled for him, which seemed to make her happy. Ryan knew I traveled to many countries when I was in college, but this is something I never knew he wanted to do as well. I am so grateful Ryan has brothers and sisters with loving and giving hearts that completely love their brother, and love him so much they are determined to make sure his dreams are fulfilled. And I know Ryan would have done the same for each of them. However, I am also just consumed with sadness that my Ryan wasn't given the opportunity, or the time, to live out his own dreams.

When I read these words I was amazed at two things. First, the fact Ryan was writing about what he wanted to do before he died struck me odd. Why would he be writing about such things within a week of his dying? But the one thing that opened my eyes, and sent me searching, is when he talked about skydiving. He said the only problem was you had to be 18 years old to skydive and he only hoped he would live that long. What 16-year-old, with his/her invincible mindset, even questions the idea of dying before reaching age 18? I KNEW then his soul somehow knew his time here would be short. Even though he didn't recognize it, at a soul level he did. It was then I realized this is so much bigger than I understood. Heaven was not enough; I needed to find Ryan! My unwavering longing to understand what was happening and my motherly need to find my son set me on the biggest journey of my life. My eyes *opened, my heart listened and my mind took in everything I could learn about the afterlife.*

The dream about my dad I had prior to Ryan's death, the dreams about Ryan, and the note I found were enough for me to realize that this world and the world after are completely connected. My dream and Ryan's journal were clear signs to me that his time was quickly coming to an end, and everyone seemed to know what was coming. My gut instinct told me to read and learn about the afterlife. I had seen enough to realize that life was going on, and my son was still very much a part of my daily life. My deep love for Ryan led me on a search to understand this. When someone you love dies, the longing is very great. When your child dies, the longing is unbearable. The need to know where he is, and how he is, consumes you. I could have sat in the darkness that surrounded me or I could begin searching. I was being given signs, messages and notes. I knew without a doubt Ryan was communicating with me. I knew someone was calling me forward on a spiritual search and journey; and in this search, the transformation within was born. As painful as it was, and still is, I would soon learn that Ryan's death was, in part, meant to be a spiritual rebirth for me. I had no idea what was about to happen.

Chapter 8

Validations

I have always believed in God. I have always believed in heaven. I grew up going to church; and no matter what pain I have faced, I never questioned the existence of God. I believed people who went before us watched over us, although I wasn't sure what that looked like. I never thought much about communicating with people on the other side. I never paid attention to mediums. I didn't judge them or what they believed; I just didn't think about it. So in that sense, when the time came to start searching, I was very open-minded about what I saw, read and heard. As time went on and validations were given to me, my openness turned into amazement, gratitude and peace. In all honesty, I feel a little scattered in my thoughts as I recall how all of my validations and gifts opened up, and I wish I would have kept a journal of them as they occurred so I had the exact order they were given to me. However, I was consumed in the emotions of what was happening, so I apologize if I come across in a scattered manner.

After I found the journal Ryan had left, I began my search to find him. In that search, I went to see John Edwards who just happened be in a town nearby. Coincidence? I think not. I had never seen a medium but knew I needed to do just that. Was it real? Could people really communicate with those who had crossed over to the other side of life to heaven?

It was an experience I will never forget! As I sat in that audience, I watched him move from person to person. Each one left in awe, laughter and/or tears. It was amazing to witness. The energy in that building was something I can't describe. It filled me and healed me for the 2 hours I sat there witnessing unbelievable things. As I walked out I remember thinking to myself: if you never believed in this before, you certainly could not leave this event and not believe now. It was the affirmation I needed. I KNEW Ryan had been sending me messages, so I needed to find a way to connect with him myself.

I began reading many books. I read books written by people who had lost a child, books written by mediums and books on near-death experiences. I couldn't seem to get enough information. I wanted to hear all opinions, experiences and beliefs. I learned about spirit guides, which was a new concept for me. I grew up believing in guardian angels; and from what I was learning, the spirit guides and guardian angels could be one and the same, different words used to describe those with the same purpose: to help protect and guide us in life. In one of my readings, I came across a meditation to connect with loved ones. I started doing this every evening as I lay in bed, and it wasn't long before doors started to open.

As I did this meditation, I began to see a white hue floating around in my vision. I saw it with my eyes closed; and when I opened my eyes, it was still there. It floated and moved around much like you would expect a spirit to do (I will refer to it as a spirit from this point on because I'm not really sure what it was I was seeing, but am pretty sure it was some type of spirit form). I KNEW it was Ryan with me. I also knew if I shared this with people they would think I was crazy or creating things out of my own desperate need. I shared this experience with very few. One evening when I was connecting I asked Ryan to give me a sign so I could be absolutely sure it really was him. No sooner had I finished that sentence and the white spirit I was seeing turned purple (Ryan's favorite color). That eliminated any doubt I had and completely validated what I had believed to be true. I was connecting with my son!

From that time on, the spirit I saw remained purple. I found myself meditating every chance I could just so I could feel close to Ryan. The next validation and opening of more spiritual doors came when I was meditating and noticed there was a green spirit moving in sync with his purple one. They moved together perfectly, like a finely choreographed dance. Instinctively I knew someone else was there with Ryan. I then asked who was with Ryan. I asked the spirit to please tell me who he was. Instantly I had a vision in front of me, words resembling a letter. It read, "It has been my honor and privilege to be

140

Ryan's guide for the past ... years." I was so startled that the letter just vanished. Could it be that I was now communicating with Ryan's spirit guide? I couldn't believe what was happening! I asked him who he was and instantly had another vision in front of me. By a vision, I mean a picture, whether it's a still shot (like the latter) or something in motion, as if you were watching TV (like this next vision). I saw a black man standing by a car. He had a huge smile on his face, a loving twinkle in his eyes, and he was looking right at me. All of a sudden he grabbed his chest, and somehow I knew he had just been shot in the chest. He then reached out and grabbed the car door as if to balance himself from falling. The vision was gone. I acknowledged that I knew he had been shot in the chest and then asked him to tell me his name. At that moment, I had a vision of my friend from work, Sandi. I saw her face, smiling as big as his, and I knew she must know this person. Instead of telling me his name, he wanted me to go through Sandi. This was bigger than just me, and it was clear messages needed to reach others. I thought to myself: how am I going to find out who this is without her thinking I'm completely insane? To be honest, I was beginning to question my own sanity.

I sent a text to Sandi the following day asking her if she knew any man who had been shot. I didn't give any details and I didn't mention where he was shot. I simply told her I had a dream that a man had been shot and he was somehow connected to her. She then told me of three people who were related to her who had been shot. Two had been shot in the chest area, so I knew the spirit had to be one of them. I then asked Sandi where they were when each had

141

been shot. I didn't want to tell her what I had seen in the vision, or that I even had a vision. Instead, I wanted -- and needed -- the validation only she could give because I thought this was all completely insane, unbelievable. I couldn't believe what was happening! I remember telling myself that if she mentioned a car I would know it was him. In the meantime, I was not going to give her any details. She told me one person had been shot by his front door, but she needed to get details on her cousin's shooting as it was a long time ago and she had forgotten the details.

I patiently waited until she finally called. She shared that her cousin had been in a fight, had walked back to his car and opened the door. Just as he was going to get in, he was shot in the chest. This was exactly what I had seen! I asked his name and she told me it was Benny. Still in doubt, I meditated that night. Sure enough, he was there again with Ryan. I asked him if I had it right and if he could please tell me his name or at least give me the first initial of his name. At that moment, I saw in front of me the words "Butch Cassidy and the Sundance Kid." Immediately afterward I heard "Benny and the Jets" singing in my ear. WOW! He probably thought I was an idiot to even ask his name after all the validations I had been given; not to mention the fact she told me it was by a car which I said would be all I need to know. Even with all of this, Benny was kind enough to make it really clear!

When Sandi called the next day she asked me why I was asking all of the questions and wanted to know what was going on. She wasn't buying that I had a dream any longer. I decided to be honest and *tell her what had happened. It was time to take a leap of faith because I knew what was happening was not insanity; it was truth. Sandi was beside herself when I told her what had happened. Come to find out, she completely believes in communication with the afterlife. How was I to know this? I was so grateful to find out because even though I knew it was real, I also knew there was a chance she would think I had lost my mind. When I told her about my last interaction with Benny and the Butch Cassidy sign I saw (because that made no sense to me), she informed me as kids they all use to call him Butch! We both about lost our minds in excitement. I could not believe what was happening, but I knew that the gifts that were opening up to me were much bigger than me. I knew they were being given to me for a reason. Benny could have easily shown me his name, just as he showed me so many other things. Instead, he showed me his cousin. He wanted to make contact with her, and she needed to know the connection we all shared and that he was still around after all of these years.*

This is so much bigger than we realize. We are more connected to people in our lives than we could even imagine. This experience was a validation that I was not creating anything out of my own need to connect with Ryan because these circumstances were not about Ryan or me; they were about Sandi and her family. My entire world was changing in ways I never could have imagined.

I shared my experience with my friend Becky because I knew she was a believer. She had lost her son about 4 years prior to Ryan's death. I remember during that time she had done some readings with a medium named Tina Powers. She was given many validations which brought her great peace. I was fascinated at the time, and it was my first exposure to a medium. Little did I know then that I would one day be calling Tina for the same reasons. Becky's pain and spiritual search for her son would be the powerful force which helped me move toward my own spiritual awakening. None of this is an accident. We are where we are and with the people we are with for a reason.

Within a year of Ryan's death, Becky had a reading with Tina during which Ryan came through. He had messages for me that Becky did not understand. When she shared them with me, I knew exactly what he was talking about, and I shared them with her. We were both amazed. Her son Lance informed her that he and Ryan were close and he had helped orchestrate our connection so we would be able to support each other. She also shared with me that Tina had told her, "When you feel a surge of energy in your body, it is often a guide or spirit confirming what you are thinking or feeling." It's like a big YES from the spirit world. This information was like another veil which was removed in my spiritual growth because I had been having energy feelings but didn't know what they meant.

Within the first year of Ryan's death he had come to a friend in dreams numerous times, bringing messages for me. He had sent many heart-shaped clouds, had come to me in my dreams, had come to me in meditations and was making his presence known through energy I felt in my body. After Becky explained what Tina had told her, I was able to ask Ryan yes or no questions and get the answers by listening to the energy level in my body. I learned a lot about what was happening with him and what was happening here. I was able to ask questions related to Becky and her son and get the answers, which Becky validated as being true answers. I felt so grateful for these gifts and the ability to communicate with my son again.

It was not long after feeling the energy of Ryan I was able to hear him speak to me. It started in dreams where we would talk to each other without speaking. It was as if we just read each other's minds, which is exactly what I had read in books about mediums and their communications, as well as near-death experiences of those who claimed to meet Jesus or family members. I was able to connect with Ryan in meditations and not only feel his energy with yes and no questions; I was hearing words. By "hearing words" I mean thoughts would just pop into my head out of nowhere and I knew it was him putting them there. At this point in time, it wasn't a sentence but merely one word conveyed. I would then try to piece it together. I would always confirm what was being said by repeating what I heard because the yes/no answers were very clear for me to hear and feel. It was my way of validating what he was saying, as opposed to recognizing my own thoughts as they came to mind. I wanted to be sure I had it right.

I then tried to connect with my dad and was so happy when I found out I could. He had messages for my mom, which I shared with her, unsure of how she would take it. I had shared a little bit of what was *happening and she listened, but I think there was skepticism as she listened, although she never expressed that. When I gave her the messages from my dad, she looked at me and said, "There is no way you could know that." I then realized from her validation I was without a doubt hearing what was being told to me. From that moment on, she would encourage me to check with Ryan or my dad about things which came up to see what they thought. My practical mother had become a believer, which I think was part of the plan since she was living with cancer at the time. Maybe this gift to her was to help make her transition home easier?*

One of my brothers, Stephen, had always felt I had some sort of gift. I had a history of having premonition-type dreams. I had also had the dream visit from my dad 2 days before Ryan's death. Stephen just felt I had some connection, and he sensed it long before I ever realized such gifts even existed. I had been sharing with him the things that had been happening, which he celebrated yet wasn't surprised by. One day I gave him messages from my dad. He believed them, but because it was about him he wanted more specific information to know it was real. He told me to ask my dad to share something that only he and my dad would know about. I remember wondering if people in the spirit world are out to prove themselves. I realized it would not be about them but rather the person who was asking. If it was important enough, I knew my dad would give me more. I checked in with him again, explaining what Stephen wanted, although I'm sure he already knew. My dad immediately told me "water." I wasn't sure what that meant so I asked him if Stephen would understand. His reply was "no," which made me laugh. I asked him to provide more details. I then had a vision of my sprinklers running in my front yard. I was very confused by this and for the next 24 hours kept checking in with my dad to see if I was to tell Stephen "sprinklers." Each time he told me yes. I'm sure if the people in the spirit world ever lose their patience, this would have been one of those times!

I finally called Stephen. Doubting myself, even though my dad kept confirming it with me, I told my brother what my dad had said to tell him. Stephen began to cry on the phone and told me he would call back. When he finally called back, he told me that the sprinklers were actually one of the fondest memories he had with my dad. While we were growing up, our family owned a resort. On occasion my dad would wake my brother up and let him go out in the darkness of early morning to help him set the sprinklers. I knew nothing about it, nor did our mom. Stephen said he never told our dad how much that meant to him, but he had shared that with his friend not long before -- a validation for Stephen (and myself) that our dad knows what's in his heart and what is happening in his life now. It was amazing for us both!

I also had mentioned many of the spiritual gifts I had been given with my friend, Sandi. Our connection had grown much deeper after we found out her cousin had been one of Ryan's guides. She would periodically ask me to check in with her dad, who often had messages for her mom. The first thing he ever asked me to tell her was "orchids." He said to tell Sandi to get her mom an orchid plant and tell her it was from him. When I shared that with Sandi, she told me that her dad would bring orchids home to his mom almost every day. She was so moved and shocked. She bought her mom an orchid plant and told her it was from her dad. Sandi said it brought so much joy to her. That's what it's all about!

The first time I actually heard a spirit speaking to me when I wasn't doing meditation was with Sandi. We had jury duty together, and her dad was in that courtroom with us. I couldn't hear what he was saying; but when we had our lunch break, he decided to join us. He was answering questions she had and confirming things for her of which I had no knowledge. I was amazed I was able to sit at a table and hear what her dad was saying as if he were sitting right there with us. I realized he WAS sitting there and my gifts were opening even more. I was so grateful. The last thing he said, and he kept saying, was "Christmas plant." Sandi had no idea what he was talking about but said she would ask her mom when she went to see her after jury duty. When Sandi got to her mom's she didn't have to ask a thing because when she walked into her mom's apartment, her mom was holding a plant and said, "Look at the new Christmas plant I just got." Sandi immediately shared what was said at lunch. Once again, her mom was filled with joy and peace knowing her husband was right there with her. Sandi couldn't believe it; and for me, it was more validation of what was happening to and through me.

Some of my greatest validations have come with my friend Becky. Through her readings, and my own, we have discovered that our boys are friends in *the afterlife and are working together and with us. We lovingly refer to them as "the boys" now. She is the one who first introduced me to mediums and readings as she shared them after she lost her son, Lance. I remember feeling so intrigued by what she was experiencing. Although I don't remember what I asked at the time, she has often told me I asked questions no one else asked. Perhaps this was because my soul knew I would be experiencing this same pain one day. Becky is also the first person with whom I shared any of my spiritual gifts. She has supported me, encouraged me and always believed in me. Even when I doubt my abilities, she stands strong. Many times she would ask me to check in with Lance about something, so I would ask. He would have messages for her, and I would relay them to her. Again, it was usually just a word or two at a time I would receive.*

Things really blossomed and grew when Becky and I flew down to Arizona for a conference on Communication with the Afterlife. It was an amazing conference with inspiring presentations. I think the most important thing for each of us happened two evenings we spent on the balcony of her room. I did a reading for her both nights and was able to give her affirmation on some pretty serious stuff that had happened when she was younger, things she had feelings about but didn't know for sure. In talking with her dad and mom, we were able to really get life-changing clarity for Becky. I was amazed at how clearly I was hearing not just words but complete thoughts attached to the feelings that came with them. I remember thinking there must be something pretty magical in the Arizona air.

On our last night we talked with our boys. At one point Lance said to watch the sky, so we did. Within 5 minutes we witnessed an amazing lightning show which went on for a long time. We had hoped for lightning the entire time we were there but did not see any until Lance told us to watch the sky. Our boys were having a great time with the electricity that night! A couple of weeks later in a reading I had, the medium was seeing flashes of light in her room. She said Ryan was saying how happy they were that we saw the lightning they sent. How could she know that? She couldn't! Another validation was given.

My doctor, and friend, Winston Vaughan, has encouraged me to create a nonprofit to help other parents. He has encouraged this since I first started giving the Ryan Depp "One Love" Scholarship Awards, which I present to two graduating seniors each year. He has even gone as far as telling me if I create this nonprofit, he will write me a check! I had thought about it, but my focus was Ryan's scholarship fund and I really didn't know how I could help other parents. Despite this, I knew Winston's words meant something and there was a reason he kept encouraging me to do this. He was part of this plan, I just knew it. I am very grateful to him. He has been supportive and loving since I first lost Ryan and now shares in the spiritual gifts I have been given. I consider him to be instrumental in the organization we are now creating.

When we came back from Arizona, Becky and I talked about opening a branch of another nonprofit group which helps grieving parents. When I told her what Winston had told me and encouraged me to do,

150

she said maybe we are suppose to start our own. She told me to check with the boys, which I did; and sure enough, she was right. Winston was right.

Since then the boys have told us the name of the organization and who we are to help. We have already helped one woman who lost her son 25 years ago. I have given her numerous readings. Following the second one, and the validations she was given during the reading, she said to me, "How can I ever thank you for giving me my son back?" That's how big this is! That is where our boys have led us. They have guided us the entire way, and presently the paperwork is sitting in Sacramento awaiting approval. Once more, validations have been given showing me not only that my son lives, but that his work is not over. He and Lance are leading us down a path where we can help many, many grieving people. We are all a team, and I believe this was part of the plan from the beginning. How powerful and amazing!

In the past couple of years I have had about seven readings with mediums whose names I have gotten from Becky or other reliable sources. I have talked with Tina Powers, Susanne Wilson and Jamie Clark. They all approach and present readings in very different manners, but they have all been very accurate in what they have told me. I could give many examples, but they would be meaningless to anyone but me. I just ask that you trust me when I say they were all the purest of validations that Ryan and my parents are very much alive and aware of what is happening in my life.

These mediums have told me things no one could possibly know. They have all told me I had psychic gifts and mediumship abilities, and they have done so without my mentioning any of the spiritual things that had happened to me. I purposely go into readings not giving any information because I want the validations to be real and true. They told me I would be doing readings for people and it would start with people I feel safe with. It would start with close friends and then expand out. That has happened.

I was told Ryan is now one of my guides, which I had a feeling about. I was told (by Ryan) that he would help me with my book and readings. He has done both. When I have done readings with my friends, Rya n is right there as I begin. I physically feel his energy in my body; that is how I know he is with me. He sends energy to my legs. I am not sure why he does that except perhaps it is a way to distinguish his energy from those of other spirits.

The mediums have told me things that had not yet happened, but were to come, and did. They told me things which made no sense at the time, but within months to follow I would clearly find out what they meant. I have learned that when I hear something that is not making sense to just tuck it away, because eventually it does make sense.

Many times a common message or symbol has been presented in the various readings. For example, a bumble bee was showing up in readings with three different mediums. It wasn't until the last reading that we figured out the bee was coming from my dad. He told us that it was his nickname when he was younger. When the medium asked me why she was seeing the nickname spelled "B-E-E" with my dad, versus simply "B," I informed her of his last name, *which is Beebout. My dad had been trying to make his presence known for three readings, and we finally figured out it was him! It has been an amazing experience and one I would highly recommend to anyone who has lost a loved one, especially someone who has lost a child.*

In January of 2014 I had a reading with Tina Powers. During the first half of the reading, my guides talked and encouraged me to write a book. I had been thinking that I was suppose to do that but had not shared it with anyone! The guides informed Tina that I already knew I needed to write a book. My blog was to be part of the book, which again was information I had not shared with Tina. This was affirmation that what I was feeling was exactly what was supposed to be happening. I learned from the reading that the quiet voice within, the one that whispers in each person's ear, is the voice we need to listen to. It is the soul which knows each one's path.

It is our guides who are trying to help us stay on our paths, and it is our loved ones who are endlessly beside us as we walk the paths we came here to walk. Since this reading, the book validation has been addressed with Jamie and Susanne, neither who knew anything about it. I was told to try and wrap it up this year while I had the momentum. It is one year this month, January 2015, and I am now finishing the book. I did it!

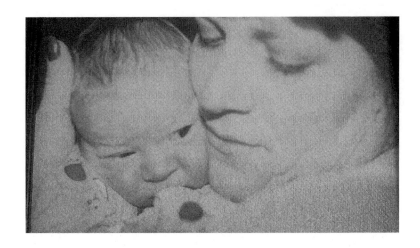

Chapter 9

Inner Peace

"Inner peace" is a pretty bold statement for someone who has lost a child. I don't know that I would say I am at peace with life and the loss I have endured, but I do have an inner peace. That doesn't mean all is right in the world, nor that I am all right with the loss of my son, because I don't think these things will ever be mine. However, knowing that Ryan is alive and with me gives me the inner peace I need to move forward on the path I was meant to walk.

When this journey began on September 22, 2010, I thought my world had just ended. I knew I would never be the same, although I didn't know what that meant. I could barely breathe. When I allowed myself to really feel the emotions of losing my 16-year-old son, I wanted to just die so I could be with him again. That feeling scared me more than I can

154

express. That overwhelming darkness was so consuming that I fought with all I had not to allow myself to feel the complete despair. I was afraid I could never get out of the darkness which surrounded me and consumed me. I was so devastated and broken within. My entire family was broken. It's a feeling that cannot be described, but anyone who has lost a child knows exactly what I'm talking about.

When I found the journal entry about skydiving I mentioned earlier in this book, I knew that this life — and the life after -- were much bigger than I understood. I knew from reading Ryan's questioning if he would live until 18 that his soul knew his time here was short. It was the beginning piece of the puzzle I knew I had to put together. I needed to understand, and the only way to do that was to find my son. Heaven was not enough anymore. I needed to find Ryan!

It was then that I began reading books on the afterlife written by many different people. One idea which seemed to be a common thread was that young people who die young are often older souls who come here to teach us something before they get to leave. Often in their dying, they continue to teach. Their actual deaths can also be tools in their teachings. For example, a young person's death can take your soul to a higher spiritual level or open doors to walk through to help others. Ryan was well beyond his years in many ways. He was a normal teenager, but his heart and soul were old. He was loving, forgiving and accepting in a way most adults could learn from. He was the kind of kid people wanted to be around, and no one had a negative thing to say about him. He *was everyone's friend. It didn't matter what walk of life a person came from, Ryan was his or her friend. What has been interesting to me is that most of the parents I have met or talked to describe their kids in the same way. That just validates for me that they were also old souls and they did what they came to do. If Ryan died to help my soul in any way, then I was going to find out what I was supposed to be learning or doing. As a mom, I was not going to let my son die in vain. If I was meant to learn something from his death, or do something as a result, then I would find out what that was. If agreements were made, I needed to stand up to my part. I was not going to let him down if part of his dying was to help me in my journey.*

I started writing my blog within weeks of Ryan's death. I have always been a very private person, especially when it came to dealing with sadness or struggles. Writing was something that came naturally to me and was often healing, so I knew I wanted to document the journey I was on to help release my emotions and to see where the journey would take me. However, I didn't know why I was feeling called to put my painful journey on a public forum. It was very foreign to share my pain where people could see it. Despite this, I knew I was meant to do it and also knew somehow, someday, some way I would understand the reason.

Through my blog I have met many people who have suffered loss of their children. I have received numerous emails from parents who felt the turmoil I was writing about in my blog. They thanked me for writing what their hearts felt. I realized at that time that the comfort they were receiving was in knowing they were not alone. Their feelings were not isolated feelings and they may survive this like I was doing. Even in the greatest of pain and grief, there is comfort in knowing you are not alone. You are surrounded by people who want to help, but the only people who really seem to be able to help are those who have shared your heartache. It's not because they have the answers; it's because they genuinely understand. Therefore, you are not alone. I assumed this must have been the reason I was led to share my journey. Four years later, I realize the blog and what it has done to help others is just the beginning of what I am being called to do. This book is also a part of the journey I am meant to be on. It is part of my work here.

Since I was in college, I have felt like I was meant to write a book. I never knew what I would write about and never believed in myself enough to do it. When I lost Ryan, I was given the painful topic. It started with my blog, and after many emails from other parents, I started to think perhaps I was meant to take the blog to a larger forum. I was meant to help more people than my blog was reaching. I didn't act on it until I was told in the reading I mentioned before that I was suppose to write a book. The book was to be about the loss and the learning to move forward (my blog), but it was also to include the spiritual things which have happened to me. There was my fear, the fear of what others would think. I was told it didn't matter because sharing the validations and experiences I have had is where the healing will be for other parents. It is more than helping others realize they are not alone; it is helping them understand that life goes on and their children are still very much alive and with them. There is the healing and inner peace I am meant to share.

I know many people have issues with those who claim to be able to communicate with people who have "died." I am not here to convince people of anything as everyone has his or her own beliefs and opinions, which I respect. I simply am sharing my journey in hopes it can help others in their healing. I have carried my experiences very privately because I was afraid of what people would think. I did not even bring it into my blog out of my own fear. I am no longer afraid. It is only now I realize it doesn't matter what others think. I know it is real. I have seen and experienced things which left me in awe and do nothing but validate that life goes on. What I find interesting is that some people who believe in God, and heaven, don't believe there can be communication with those who have died. It's almost seen as an evil to some, which I find very sad. Jesus talked to people after his death. He rose from the dead, and He showed us life goes on and communication is possible. He showed us this. Why do we question others being able to do this? Are not all things possible with God? I believe they are. The Bible talks about spiritual gifts, and I believe communication with the afterlife is a spiritual gift. I feel blessed, showered in God's grace and ready to stand up and own what has been given to me. I thank God for this gift. It has saved not only me but my entire family. I have no doubt it will bring great healing to others as well.

By sharing my story I hope to help bring healing to other parents. I genuinely feel that is part of the plan for me on this earth. I know the loss is devastating. I'm not going to say that I don't feel sadness still, because I do. There are times that I still feel hopeless, and the longing to have Ryan here is all I can think of. Every holiday that passes, every birthday I celebrate without him, every anniversary of his death, every milestone one of his friends surpasses and every time our family is all together, I painfully feel his absence. There are times when I would give back all of my gifts and spiritual awakenings to just hold Ryan in my arms. Having him here with me again would be the one thing that would make my world right again and fill my heart with complete peace. But that can't happen. He is done with this life here. He did what he came to do and returned Home. Now I am left here to finish my job -- our job -- and I must do it.

The inner peace I have been given comes from the knowledge that Ryan is still very much alive. Not only that, he is very much a part of my life. When we lose a child, or anyone for that matter, the individual continues to watch over us and help us. He/she knows what is happening in our lives, and those are the validations you can get in readings. Our loved ones want so desperately for us to know they are still here. They send signs and validations all of the time. I can only imagine how many signs are sent that are left unseen or unheard. Every missed sign is healing that is not being received. All we have to do is open our eyes and listen with our hearts.

I have two new and very dear friends who lost their daughter, Kayla, just over a year ago. She is a sweet girl who I have had the honor of connecting with. Kayla's mom, Kris, started seeing signs from her immediately. Kayla's favorite color was pink, and I can't tell you how many pink sunsets Kris has seen since her death. She knows it's Kayla, and Kayla validated that for her. Kayla has given me messages for her mom and dad. Some made sense immediately and others made sense at a later date. One time she wanted me to tell her dad, Mike, "bobby pin." Neither of us was sure why. It wasn't long after he was on his boat -- a boat filled with memories of Kayla -- that he looked on the floor and there lay a bobby pin! He instantly knew this is what the message was about and she was there. Kayla knew it was there, knew he would get on that boat again, and wanted him to be sure and know that when he saw the bobby pin, she would be right there with him. It worked! The messages are healing and give hope. They validate the faith that life goes on. The signs she has sent both of them have done the same.

As parents, we need the healing and hope if we are going to survive the greatest loss any human being can endure. If you see something or hear a song and immediately think of that person you lost, chances are that sign or song was sent just for you. When Ryan died, I saw heart-shaped clouds all the time and had never seen them before. The first time I saw one I thought of him immediately and just knew it was him. I was right. I have read many books that told of people who shared stories of seeing signs -- ladybugs, dragon flies or butterflies -- from their children. They all recognized the signs, but they didn't take it further. Signs are the beginning of the communication, and actual conversations can happen if you choose to seek it out. They want so badly to talk with us and are so very happy when we see the signs and know it's them!

I have talked a lot with Becky about the gifts we have both been given, the most important being the communication we are able to have with our boys. We have often talked of not understanding how any parent can survive without the knowledge that his or her child is still alive and with him/her. We have shared many tears together. We have tried to hide our pain from each other. We each remember the despair and can't imagine being trapped in that darkness. My heart aches for these parents. It is hard enough to survive when you know they are with you because even that doesn't seem like enough sometimes. It is my sincere hope that this book can help heal the hearts of parents who don't know their children are still with them.

It has been a long road to get here, but I am here. I know there will be times I don't feel the peace inside, as I already have those days. I know there will always be times I don't want to face the day without Ryan, because I already have those days. I know there will be times the sadness will slip in and make me feel like I've taken 100 steps backwards from where I've come. But I also know I will get back on my feet and remember how blessed I am to know my son is right beside me and working with me as I finish this life on earth.

In every pain we face in this life there is something to learn from it. As the saying goes, there is a silver lining in every cloud. I know earth-shattering heartache. I know the unbearable pain of losing a child. I know the unspeakable torment of getting up each day when your heart has been destroyed by the loss of someone who is so much a part of who you are. I know the empty feeling of life as you face it each day with such a painful void so deep in your heart. I know the all-consuming loneliness within as you look at the world knowing it could never be the same as it was before. I know the sadness in not remembering what joy feels like. I know darkness, heartbreak and anguish. Through God's grace I have come to know other things.

I now know without a doubt Ryan lives. I know he is with me and loving me more than I could even imagine. I know he walks beside me and tries to help me through each day. I know he sees the bigger picture and is leading me on the path I am meant to walk. I know he speaks from a place of pure truth, so I listen to all he shares with me. I know he sees my life's plan and helps guide me to do what I came here to do. I know he wants me to be happy. I know he is proud of how far I have come and all I am doing to bring good out of this pain. I know he will never leave me. I know he sees how hard I am trying. I know one day I will be with him again. I know when it's my turn to go, he will be the first one there to welcome me home with his arms open wide. I look forward to the day I see that big smile of his and hopefully hear him say, "You did a great job, Mom!"

I sincerely hope that in sharing my journey I can help other parents who are grieving the loss of their children. My wish in sharing my pain -- my attempts in moving forward, the validations I have been given along the way, and the inner peace I have found as a result -- is that it will somehow help open other parents' hearts to receive the same. My prayer is that every parent will see the signs his/her child sends, because I guarantee they ARE sending signs! I pray that communication with your child comes as a result of these signs. I pray that all parents can find some good out of their tragedy so they learn what they need to learn, in order to finish what they came here to do. Your children will be helping you! Lastly, I pray that this book will somehow start a ripple effect, spreading the hope, faith and love which our children are sending us each and every day -- the greatest of these gifts: LOVE.

WE did it Ryan!

AMVets
2 - 28 - 2022

80505919R00092

Made in the USA
Lexington, KY
03 February 2018